CONFLICT, MEETINGS, AND DIFFICULT PEOPLE

The Essential Guide for Members of California's
Public Boards, Town Councils, Commissions,
Agency Staff, and Neighborhood Associations

Barry Phegan, PhD, Author of *Developing Your Company Culture*

Dedicated to civic leaders who want
more-effective ways to resolve community conflicts.

CONFLICT, MEETINGS, and DIFFICULT PEOPLE

The Essential Guide for Members of California's Public Boards, Town Councils, Commissions, Agency Staff, and Neighborhood Associations

Copyright © 2018 by Barry Phegan

AMBIENCE PRESS

Contact barry@ambiencepress.com

ISBN: 978-1-7322483-0-4

To order this book visit www.ambiencepress.com

Manufactured in the United States of America

FOREWORD

This guide contains tools to manage conflict, meetings and difficult people. The tools come from almost two thousand commissioners, public board members, town council members and public officials attending University of California Extension workshops, and from my thirty years of working with managers in the public and private sector, building teams and organizations with great trust, cooperation and satisfaction.

Members of boards, commissions, town councils and agency staff across California (and nationally) struggle with managing conflict and participation—particularly in public meetings, which are often messy and frustrating.

Most civic leaders experience this frustration. If you bring some of the tools in this guide to your fellow board, council, or commission members, they might thank you. Your meetings will be more effective—and you'll be happier.

Some ideas and tools in this guide will fit your beliefs as well as your city, town, county, or region; others will seem outlandish. Use what feels right.

Barry Phegan, PhD
Marin County, California
barry@ambiencepress.com

CONTENTS

4. WORKING WITH DIFFICULT PEOPLE · 73

5. APPENDIX · 91

WORDS, WORDS, WORDS

"When I use a word," Humpty Dumpty said <u>in</u> rather a scornful tone, "it means just what I choose it to mean—neither more nor less."

"The question is," said Alice, "whether you can make words mean so many different things."

"The question is," said Humpty Dumpty, "which is to be master—that's all."

Lewis Carroll, Through the Looking Glass

(Remember? Later on Humpty took a great fall!)

"Commission" – "Public Board" – "Town Council"

This book uses the word "commission" loosely. It can mean "town council" or "public board" such as a school board; a county board of supervisors; a county or state commission, agency or department; or a neighborhood association.

"Commissioner" means a person elected or appointed to such a "Commission," who resolves public concerns in a public forum such as a town council meeting, a planning commission meeting, board of supervisors, school board or neighborhood meeting.

Note: On "Chairperson"

When the book uses the word "chairperson" or "chair," it does not necessarily mean the formally designated lead person on a commission or board—or the mayor. Whenever a group member takes the role of **process leadership**, he or she is acting as informal chairperson (*Page 17*).

For example, if you ask the commission, "If it's OK by you, before we discuss actions, could we ask how commissioners and members of the public experience the problem personally?" you are then guiding the commission's process, thereby making yourself the informal chairperson.

"His" – "Her" – "Their"

We have an unfortunate cultural legacy of male dominance; a patriarchal culture and language. In this book you'll find sentences using his, her, his/her, his or her, and their. Truth is, I got tired of typing and proofing "his or her." Perhaps, like me, many readers recognize the desirability of correct gender usage but find it can be repetitive and boring, while often obscuring sentence simplicity. Please tolerate any inconsistencies and incorrectness.

MACHIAVELLI

This guide helps you reduce conflict and build cooperation. If you enjoy using your Commissioner position for *Game-of-Thrones*-style power and combat, stop here and read Machiavelli's *The Prince*.

I don't discuss how to use lies and the media to destroy your opponents, as sometimes happens with large state, county or regional commissions, and big-city councils. Such raw brutality contributes to the polarization and cynicism we experience today. While competition and dominance may gratify certain (sociopathic?) individuals, it doesn't build healthy communities *(Page 84)*.

This guide advocates for my optimistic view that with the right information and tools, good people do good work.

HISTORY OF THIS GUIDE

This Guide grew from day-long workshops that were first offered through the University of California Berkeley, University Extension. Most early participants were planning commissioners. Other groups soon joined, as word spread that the class was a great place to meet peers and take home useful, pre-tested ideas from other commissioners. Most UC campuses offered the class. At UC Irvine, class sizes sometimes exceeded 200.

One of the amusing (maybe?) consequences of this popularity was that several complete town councils might sign up, providing an opportunity to discuss the Brown Act *(Page 97)* and the possible illegality of what we were doing right there in class. It was an example of one of the more difficult issues confronting public officials—building trust and normal human working relationships in a legal setting presupposing adversarial or illicit behavior.

Workshop members raised concerns that they were uncomfortable discussing with fellow commissioners—and would certainly not be comfortable discussing in public. They cited problems they inadvertently created by publicly voicing their personal position on issues before the commission *(Pages 64–67)* and their pain managing polarized audiences.

Before the class, few of these commissioners realized that they were locked into an adversarial culture, a legal system and problem-resolution process that began with divisiveness on solutions, rather than exploring the common ground of people's experience, assumptions and beliefs around the underlying issues or problems.

Class participants often disagreed on the usefulness or validity of what members from other communities found normal and workable. This was particularly true with interpretations of the Brown Act, and the management of relationships between commissions or boards and agency staff.

Most attendees were from local government. This is often reflected in suggestions.

ACKNOWLEDGEMENTS

Almost two thousand dedicated town council members and elected and appointed town commissioners and public board members contributed to this guide. Thank you all.

My thanks also to Paul Leinberger who initiated the UC Berkeley Extension workshops that inspired this guide, and my friends and associates who generously contributed information and suggestions, to Bill Ahern for observations on state level power politics, to Jack Nixon who expanded the guide's audience, and to Don Bradley who helped shape the review process. Cartoons are by Tim McGee. Rosina Wilson edited the manuscript.

Errors and omissions I claim as my own.

Barry Phegan, PhD
Marin County, California
barry@ambiencepress.com

X |

Section 1

THE SIERRA MEADOWS STORY

THE SIERRA MEADOWS STORY

This short story introduces the tools in this guide. It describes one commissioner's search for a better way. While the characters and the town are fictional, the story is based on actual situations, problems and results I have witnessed in my more than thirty years of working with "commissions" at all levels of government.

This story has a happy ending. Will yours?

Barry Phegan

Claire Conner

Claire Conner (fictional) chairs the Sierra Meadows (fictional) Planning Commission in Placer County, California. Four years ago, a Los Angeles developer bought rights to a tract adjoining the town. They plan a resort with ski runs, hotels, stores, condominiums and possibly a casino. They want to be annexed by Sierra Meadows.

Residents are not up in arms. They know what's happening. Their concerns are heard. They trust that the resort will be good for them and their community. How did that happen? Here's Claire's story. *(She appears again on pages 49–50 and 84.)*

Lead by Example

The Conner family settled in the area in 1846 during the gold rush. Claire grew up on the family farm, five miles north of the present town, where she learned that while you can push animals around with a stick, leading them with a carrot works better. As a mother she found it was the same at home. After years of shouting at her two boys, and not getting results, she learned to lead them by example.

When her boys were in high school, Claire stepped into local politics, because the school board wasn't focused on the children. Members had their own agendas, argued in public, held chaotic meetings with disorganized agendas, and made confused decisions. They couldn't manage public participation. What people said seemed irrelevant to them. From this, Claire saw how not to run public meetings.

Involve People Who Are Affected

Claire manages the local organic dairy. She began twelve years ago on the loading dock, where she learned some leadership basics. Her supervisor's decisions seemed mostly good, but sometimes felt off-the-wall to her. She realized that if he had involved her in his decisions, or in carrying them out—even a little bit—she'd have contributed some good ideas and certainly felt better.

Four years ago, Claire joined the Sierra Meadows Planning Commission, becoming its chair two years later. She was eager to apply the two leadership lessons: lead by example and involve the people affected by a decision in the decision. She invited the other four commissioners to her house for once-a-month Thursday meetings to discuss how they might better manage and lead the commission.

They needed clearance from the town's attorney because commission meetings must be publicly noticed. Claire knew they couldn't discuss managing themselves in public. It would be like opening your family to strangers. It wouldn't work.

The town's attorney came to their first meeting and was satisfied that they were not violating the Brown Act *(Page 97)*. Claire did a barbecue. It took several meetings for the five of them to open up, build trust and discuss who they were as commissioners. Now they have a real team. It's visible at their public meetings.

Manage the Situation

After high school, Claire attended Sierra College. She remembers a psychology professor saying that if you want to understand why people do what they do, first look at their situation *(Page 16)*. Our situation tells us what to do. If it's cold, you put on a sweater. If a good friend dies, you are sad. You are always you, but what you do depends on your situation.

Claire discussed with her fellow commissioners how their situation created conflict, asking what could they change to reduce conflict. The group concluded that their situation had three fairly distinct sources of conflict: themselves, other governmental groups, and their applicants and public.

While they had most control over the first piece, themselves, they had conflicting views of their job, and their personalities sometimes rubbed each other the wrong way. Fortunately, they got through these early discussions without biting each other's heads off. It wasn't easy.

One commission member, Moose Ormsby, had recently arrived from the Bay Area. He'd picked up some useful ideas at a workshop he had attended at UC Berkeley, University Extension, "How to Be a More Effective Public Commissioner or Board Member."

(Mis)Understanding Ourselves

His first insight was that many interpersonal conflicts come from one person misunderstanding another's intentions. We each have different ways of seeing problems and making decisions. If one person doesn't understand another person's approach, they may misunderstand and get frustrated, or even angry.

Moose brought an inventory from the workshop handbook *(Page 19)*. Members marked words that best described themselves, then looked at associated words showing how another person might misunderstand. For example, an "organizing" person might be seen by others as "controlling."

The commissioners each did the exercise and they compared results. It helped them understand each other better, smoothing over irritations that might otherwise be visible in public meetings. It also helped them understand problems that they might have when working with "difficult" people.

Manage Related Government Agencies

Along with reducing conflict among themselves, the commissioners built trust and understanding with groups they depended on, especially those that control them: the Sierra Meadows Town Council and the Planning and Community Development Department.

Other government agencies they work with indirectly include the Placer County Board of Supervisors, some state and regional agencies such as Caltrans and the Tahoe Regional Planning Agency, and some federal agencies, such as the US Environmental Protection Agency.

Claire knew that establishing trusting relationships with these groups would reduce potential conflicts, making her commission more effective.

The commissioners listed the key people in these local agencies. There were about twenty five. Each commissioner hosted one coffee or lunch meeting a month, completing the list in six months.

Now those people and agencies better understand the planning commission, what it wants and how it works, particularly the values they want to show in Sierra Meadows. Today, when there is a conflict or an issue—going in either direction—it's usually resolved with a phone call or text message.

Each commissioner also met with every person in the Planning and Community Development Department, inviting each staff member out for coffee or lunch. Now they know each other personally and enjoy working together. There's minimal conflict.

Managing Applicants and Meeting Attendees

The third important group was the planning applicants and people attending commission meetings. While a Commission has very little control over who these people are and what they bring, they have complete control over how they will respond, particularly **how the commission sets the discussion and decision stage to reduce conflict**.

Claire's commission realized they were stuck in an adversarial public-hearing process that encouraged conflict *(Page 40)*. Citizens came before them arguing positions for or against something, seeing the commission as judge. The commission met in the town council's chambers, sitting behind a panel bench on a raised platform—like a miniature Supreme Court. In addition, they had to comply with the Brown Act, which presupposes illegal and corrupt activity.

The commission recognized that it was a perfect stage for battle. No wonder they had a serious problem with conflict. They brought it on themselves. If you used that process at home you'd land in a divorce court, yet they used it making community decisions. **If you use an adversarial process, expect conflict. It's as simple as that.**

It was several months before that insight sank in, even longer before they made conflict-reducing changes.

Rearrange the Room

They started by physically reorganizing their public meeting room *(Page 74)*. They bought five high chairs, like bar stools with backs, putting them to the side of the town council chamber dais. There were several large TV screens on the walls behind and to one side of the dais. Now they had a triangle, with the public facing the screens and the commission to the side, facing the public and the screens.

In a traditional layout, the public focuses on the commission, trying to convince them by arguing for or against particular positions. The new arrangement focused public attention on the screens, which the commission used to manage information, discussions and decisions.

The town's maintenance department built the commission a small extension to the town council dais. It is a bench-like table for papers and laptops—essential for managing discussions. There is no front panel, just as there is none in front of the public. The no-panel signals, "We are open."

After changing the seating, the commission changed their decision process.

Managing Conflict in Decisions

Previously, the commission used the traditional argumentative public process, and then voted. That left some unhappy people who later undermined decisions. It was frustrating, inefficient and divisive, working against good community. But everyone was used to it and saw no alternative—until Moose Ormsby pulled another jewel from his UC class handbook, the *4-Step Decision Process (Page 46)*.

Before using that decision process, the commission meetings—particularly the public-hearing section—were a mishmash of problems, solutions, alternatives, anxieties, imaginations, anger, fears and confusion. Now Claire can't imagine meeting without it.

First Describe the Problem

The first step asks, "What is the situation or problem?" That might seem obvious. It's not. At public meetings, the 4-Step Decision Process is displayed on the wall and on a TV screen *(Page 101)*. Claire introduces it saying:

"We use the 4-Step Decision Process, described in our Commission Public-Information Pamphlet (Page 54). That's by the door, if you don't have one already. The first step in the process is describing the situation or problem. We won't discuss what we might do until we get clear on the issues and problems as everyone here sees them."

Until commissioners realized they should build a clear picture of the situation, they had people arguing about what to do, when they had never agreed on what they were doing something about. It was as if some people in the room thought the game was football, while others were dressed for water polo.

They had always done it that way. Nobody saw how crazy that was until Moose introduced the 4-Step Decision Process. It was so simple and obvious.

Moose said the UC instructor joked that we have so many lawyers per square foot in the United States because **we jump too quickly to action—and fighting over what to do—before agreeing on the problem** *(Page 82)*.

With the 4-Step Process, everybody's problems are written down so that people can understand each other's issues. Then, rather than seeing others as opponents, they see they are all in the same boat: they're all people with problems. This clarifies issues, simplifies decisions and reduces conflict. People discuss what to do from a new perspective.

To do this, the commission uses one large overhead TV screen. The person facilitating, usually the chair, listens carefully. Using her laptop, Claire types a few key words, not sentences, onto the screen. It took her three or four meetings to get comfortable. She found that there were not many problems—rarely over twenty, usually less than a dozen.

Moose had another inventory from that UC class *(Page 42)*, showing that different people prefer different parts of that 4-Step Decision Process. The commissioners each did the exercise and compared results. Now they understand each other better, and they understand why some members of the public might feel frustrated at certain steps.

Provide More Information

In addition to reorganizing the room and their decision process, the commission now provides as much accurate information ahead of meetings as they can. They avoid wasting meeting time giving background information. Their meetings are designed for listening, discussing and deciding.

At commission meetings they have two handouts. First is the *Commission Public Information Pamphlet (Page 54),* which describes the commission, the agenda, the decision process—and how to participate. Second is the *Commission Summary Report (Page 55),* a one-page summary of any big issue before the commission.

This summary report uses the same 4-Step Decision Process, listing: 1. the issues or problems (as one-liners) and 2. the major action alternatives—and then 3. the factors to consider when evaluating those alternatives, like traffic, legality, community support, school, timing, etc.

As the commission publicly works through those three steps, one alternative usually looks most promising. Because the discussion includes every affected group, the final decision is often a consensus.

Meeting Evaluation and Feedback

Six months after introducing the 4-Step Decision Process, the commission began asking the public for feedback: *"How are we doing? How can we improve?"*

Claire and her commissioners used suggestions from written and verbal evaluations to improve their meetings *(Page 62).* Current evaluations show high levels of "customer satisfaction" with the changes they've made.

Managing Difficult People

Even though they eliminated most conflict by reorganizing the room, distributing information, involving all interest groups (using the 4-Step Decision Process) and responding to meeting evaluations, they still have a few angry people at meetings. An open decision process like this is easily abused. It's like democracy. An open culture invites uncertainty and chaos.

Most commissions and public agencies control uncertainty and chaos using Robert's Rules of Order, a semi-autocratic decision process. Claire's commission doesn't adhere to Robert's Rules, because it often brings more conflict.

This commission found that it's hard to manage difficult people in an open decision process. They needed expert coaching, fortunately finding help from the community. This remains a problem area.

When someone personally attacks a commissioner, accusing him or her of, say, being in the pocket of a developer, the note-taker—usually the chair—takes a couple of deep breaths and a sip of water, types what was said onto the overhead TV screen, smiles, looks at the person and says, "Anything else?" *(Words That Work, Page 77,* and *Argue to Win or Argue to Learn, Page 84).*

The first time Claire tried that in public, she was stunned at the effect. The accuser stopped dead in his tracks. Some of the public giggled. How often do you see a government official listen carefully and type such a statement on an overhead TV? Everyone paid attention. Non-defensiveness demonstrates respect and trust.

But such openness takes courage, practice and confidence. They didn't get there overnight. They are good at it now. The public appreciates non-argumentative commission meetings that demonstrate good community values, like listening, openness and empathy.

With emotional, difficult people *(Page 87)*, the commissioners keep in mind that nobody behaves in an unreasonable way—from their point of view. They patiently help that person clearly describe their problem, building it into the decision. Behind an emotion is usually an important issue.

The commissioners don't take people's emotions personally *(Page 85)*. Many people bring their home problems, their frustrations at work—or with the national political scene—into meetings. Claire understands, sometimes having to catch herself. She commented, "We are all human—fortunately."

Invite Your Community to Help

The Sierra Meadows Planning Commission still has occasional Thursday meetings. Sometimes they invite a local expert. The town has retired psychologists, university professors, business leaders, and managers from all levels of the private sector and government, who are eager to help—if invited.

One explained the difference between the adversarial decision process, which most commissions use, and the consensus decision process, which expresses better values and brings better decisions *(Page 40)*.

The commission has a way to go managing conflict, but it is moving in the right direction. If you attend one of their public meetings, you'll see that their community agrees.

Summary

People in Sierra Meadows and adjoining towns notice the Planning Commission's success. They see how the commissioners create consensus decisions that stick, while avoiding the adversarial process that the governmental system, and ironically the Brown Act, both encourage. They ask, "How?"

Claire suggests, first realize that what people do depends on their situation. Everyone behaves appropriately—from their own point of view. So manage your situation to make cooperation appropriate while minimizing conflict *(Page 16)*. Start at home. Build an open, trusting team of commissioners, board members or town council. Get to know each other. Discuss managing yourselves. Agree on what values you'd like to show as you work, and what that means in practice. Get legal approval for such special discussions.

Claire's commissioners have two goals: first, to deal efficiently and fairly with the substantive issues coming before them, e.g., the permits and plans; and second, contributing to a stronger community by the values they show in the way they do these things.

When discussing values, the commission concluded that most people want to contribute, be appreciated, and feel valuable and constructive. People enjoy working in groups with good relations, trust, openness, and teamwork. We each appreciate recognition, as well as going home knowing we did a good job. There's also the golden rule: Treat others the way you like being treated. And listen more than you talk. It's that old saying, "We have two ears and one mouth."

Good commission leadership is as much how you do things as what you do *(Page 39)*. How you act shows your values. Ask your commissioners, board, or council what values they'd like to see shown by their community leaders. The Sierra Meadows commissioners wrote down the values they each wanted. They still follow that list.

Claire mentions values at every planning commission meeting. It's one reason people trust the commission. They know the commissioners are trying to do the right thing for Sierra Meadows. They see that their town's in good hands.

Think about your public meetings as the stage where you play out your commissioner roles and the public plays out theirs. That stage largely controls what everyone does. Claire's commission shifted that stage from conflict to cooperation. So can you.

List the key people and organizations you rely on. Develop personal relationships with them so that they know you and trust you.

Work with your department's staff, agreeing on how you will work together—particularly your roles and responsibilities *(Page 32)*. Use the *Commission Public-Information Pamphlet*, the *Commission Summary Report* and the 4-Step Decision Process.

Claire ends with a caution.

"Don't try to do this quickly. It sounds simple, but it's far from easy. Take small steps. It took us two difficult years to get here. Now I can't imagine going back. **We shifted the field from conflict to cooperation.** *It's one of the most rewarding things I've ever done."*

Section 2

MANAGING CONFLICT

CONFLICT — WHAT IS IT?

Conflict has two general meanings:
1. **Difference**—of opinion, ideology, view or belief.
2. **Fight**—usually because of miscommunication or misinformation.

Conflict is good when the act of discussing differences leads to both parties' understanding of each other's views, thereby expanding their own. Conflict is bad when differences lead to battle *(Page 84)*.

As a commissioner or board member, your objective is not to prevent, suppress or wish away conflict, but to use it to the commission's, public's and staff's advantage.

Conflict is natural and unavoidable. Conflict is resolved in four general ways. Numbers **1.** and **2.** below, involve dominance and submission; Numbers **3.** and **4.** encourage understanding and progress.

1. **WITHDRAWAL.** One party voluntarily withdraws his perspective or view. When he gives up all ground and turns belly up, his input is lost to the system. For example:
Bill: "I think we should go for the proposal as is."
Susan: "I think we shouldn't approve it."
Bill: "OK, either way is fine. Let's drop it. I'm easy."

2. **ADVERSARIAL.** A battle for dominance, as in the courts. Part of the opposing view may be retained, but one view is dominant. Resentment and obstruction may emerge as new problems.

3. **DIALOGUE.** Both parties exchange their points of view. Communication is opened, though both retain their initial positions in a stand-off.

4. **SYSTEMS APPROACH.** Parties exchange information, explore with each other what lies behind their views and goals, bring others into the discussion to help **look for common ground** and mutually beneficial solutions and learn how the environment is supporting the conflict.

Conflict escalates when people harden their positions, narrow their communications and don't talk with each other.

Conflict is eased when people explore their positions, open up lines of communications and involve others; and while acknowledging differences, focus on common ground.

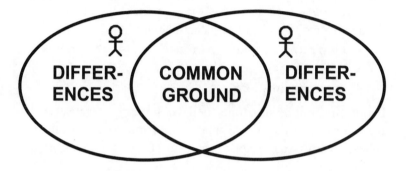

To reduce conflict, manage the situation. Organize your commission to encourage the systems approach.

MANAGING THE CONFLICT SITUATION

We each respond appropriately to our situation—from our own point of view. Our behavior is therefore information about our situation.

If there is conflict in a meeting, examine the meeting's structure and process. This is the part that you as commissioners have control over and can change.

- Don't focus on the person as if they are the problem.
- Don't look at the problem as if it is an event independent of its situation.

People in similar situations behave similarly because they share a common sense of what is appropriate. In meetings, we each know what is appropriate and how we should act.

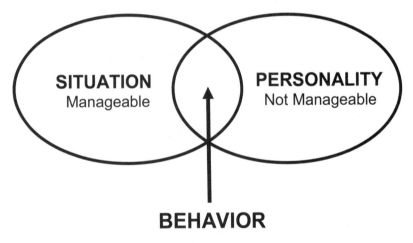

SITUATION
Manageable

PERSONALITY
Not Manageable

BEHAVIOR

Personality plays a role in what happens, but as a commissioner you can't change someone's personality—and you probably shouldn't try. **If people are arguing, it is because the situation tells them that arguing is appropriate.**

To reduce conflict, make arguing and conflict less appropriate. Look at yourselves, your processes and your meetings. Ask, "How can we as commissioners create a situation that reduces conflict and encourages cooperation?"

THE COMMISSIONER'S ROLE

As a commissioner, you often state your opinion or expertise on the particular problem or issues before the commission. This is your substantive role. There is another commissioner role—managing and leading the commission's decision and administrative process.

Managing is often defined as the process of achieving planned results **through others.** Like the football coach, the manager does not play, but he or she is responsible for results. Commissioners balance these two roles, leading both issues and process.

When making decisions and gathering data, you as a commissioner are not carrying out your process responsibilities. Many commissioners spend most of their time thinking about and expressing their personal opinions on issues. Few spend much time or thought on their commission process responsibilities.

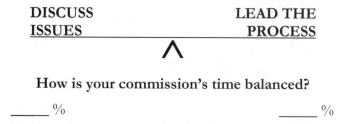

DISCUSS ISSUES   **LEAD THE PROCESS**

How is your commission's time balanced?

_____ %   _____ %

Though a commissioner's role as an independent, substantive problem solver is encouraged by law, by tradition, by staff and by peers, some commissioners step back to orchestrate the overall work of the commission hearings and staff. For these commissioners, integrating the work of peers and staff into the broader objectives of the commission and community is exciting, challenging and deeply rewarding.

Who conducts or leads your commission?

YOUR PERSONAL COMMISSIONER STRENGTHS

This inventory will help you better understand the strengths you use as a commissioner or board member.

INSTRUCTIONS:
DO NOT TURN OVER THIS PAGE UNTIL YOU HAVE COMPLETED THE EXERCISE BELOW.

Draw a circle around the eight (8) words that you believe best describe you as a commissioner or board member. The results will be most useful if you think specifically about yourself on the job, in your role as a commissioner. **Select words describing how you actually behave, NOT how you think you should behave or would like to behave. There are no preferred answers.**

Trusting	Self-Confident	Optimistic
Purposeful	Practical	Ambitious
Loyal	Idealistic	Economical
Organizing	Methodical	Helpful
Persuasive	Forceful	Analytic
Modest	Principled	Imaginative
Orderly	Fair	Supportive
Competitive	Accepting	Persevering
Adaptable	Thorough	Risk-taking

When you have circled your eight most descriptive words, turn the page and circle those same words on the chart.

THREE COMMISSIONER STYLES

1. FEELING ALTRUISTIC-SUPPORTIVE		2. ACTING ASSERTIVE-DIRECTIVE		3. THINKING ANALYTIC SELF-RELIANT	
The drive to be genuinely helpful to others.		The drive to achieve in the face of competition.		The drive for personal integrity and self-reliance.	
Typical strengths	But might be seen as	Typical strengths	But might be seen as	Typical strengths	But might be seen as
Trusting	Gullible	Self-Confident	Arrogant	Thorough	Obsessive
Optimistic	Wishful	Purposeful	Opportunistic	Practical	Unimaginative
Loyal	Slavish	Ambitious	Ruthless	Economical	Stingy
Idealistic	Unrealistic	Organizing	Controlling	Persevering	Stubborn
Helpful	Self-denying	Persuasive	Pressuring	Methodical	Rigid
Modest	Without pride	Forceful	Dictatorial	Analytic	Nit-picking
Adaptable	Unprincipled	Risk-taking	Gambler	Principled	Unbending
Accepting	Passive	Imaginative	Dreamer	Orderly	Compulsive
Supportive	Submissive	Competitive	Combative	Fair	Unfeeling
___ Total Column 1.		___ Total Column 2.		___ Total Column 3.	

WHAT DO YOUR RESULTS MEAN?

The qualities you circled work for you. For you, these behaviors are familiar and successful. You are comfortable using them.

If you score 5 or more in one column, you probably use most of the other qualities in that same column. However, be aware that people might see you differently than you see yourself, especially if they score low in that same column.

Our actions have many motives, and many meanings to others. For example, **analytic** behavior might be seen by someone else as **nit-picking**, especially if the analytic behavior is strong. Similarly, **adaptable** behavior might be interpreted as **unprincipled**.

Misunderstanding or misperceiving like this is common, particularly if the other person does not use the strength (in other words, is uncomfortable with that behavior).

In stressful situations, we may use familiar behaviors more intensely. If the other person's misperception of our behavior is a problem, then by using our strength more, we might unwittingly escalate an argument.

Turn This Around

Think of a work associate, maybe a fellow commissioner, whose behavior gives you difficulty, or makes you uncomfortable or annoyed. Look at the "Three Commissioner Styles" chart. Are there any words in the "But might be seen as" columns describing the behavior you don't like? Mark those.

Now look at the corresponding positive words on the left side of those negative words (in the "Typical strengths" columns). Try hard to imagine that the person is really behaving positively, and not as you see them with the right-hand negative word.

Almost nobody is deliberately **arrogant** or **ruthless**. Rather, they are more likely trying to be **self-confident** or **ambitious**. It may be that your misperception is the problem.

INFLUENCING OTHERS

To work more effectively with others, be aware of these potential crossed wires.

If you sense the other person is strong in:

1. FEELING (Altruistic-Supportive)

Tap their developmental strength. "Can you help me with this problem?" Appeal to high standards. Point out the benefits to be gained for others.

• Provide opportunities for keeping in touch.

• Help him/her (who doesn't want to frustrate you or hurt your feelings) in voicing concerns. Realize that open conflict is difficult for him or her and might be avoided, even at the expense of not reaching the best solution to the problem.

If I'm 1. Because of potential hurt to others, we could end up not making decisions.

If I'm 2. Watch my own tendency to overwhelm or run over. Might be impatient with **F**'s over-consideration.

If I'm 3. Might be annoyed with **F**'s concerns for others' feelings, or be impatient over meeting "just to keep in touch."

If you sense the other person is strong in:

2. ACTING (Assertive-Directive)

• Assign work needing to be done quickly or forcefully.

• Lay out your plan quickly, with the "meat" of it in the first two paragraphs.

• Stand up and be firm, but don't fight. Own your own statements: "I see the merit in your point, but in my judgment, we need to consider other things first."

• Be ready for him to take over your idea and run with it.

If I'm 1. Standing up and staying active in the conflict may be hard.

If I'm 2. Avoid the fight: take an **F** person with me to keep track of the interaction; avoid going with the first idea.

If I'm 3. Be aware of giving too many details, too much background.

If you sense the other person is strong in:

3. THINKING (Analytic Self-Reliant)

- Do your homework. Be ready for practical, hard questions.

- Make use of their logical, step-by-step approach. Give them the task of putting the plan in order.

- Agree on time limitations.

- Give them tasks to research.

- If you meet resistance, ask extensional questions. "Exactly what will happen over the next six months if we put our plan into effect?"

If I'm 1. Be aware that my need to keep in touch may not be shared. Provide some structure to meetings. Don't let over-concreteness throw me off.

If I'm 2. Avoid becoming impatient; do my homework; be aware of my wanting to jump ahead more quickly; take a **T** person with me if dealing with data is difficult for me.

Take an **F** with me if my impatience might lead me to push ahead and provoke the **T's** "stubbornness."

If I'm 3. Watch out for analysis paralysis.

ORIENTING NEW COMMISSIONERS

Without proper orientation, it takes about eighteen months for a new commissioner to feel comfortable in the role. Cities and counties use many different ways to reduce this lost time. Here are some used by several California cities.

- Get all commissioners in one room for ninety minutes discussion with Council, Attorney, Mayor, City Manager, Clerk, and Budget officer.

- Conduct a yearly orientation by the relevant staff.

- Experts give two hour seminars every six weeks. Anyone can attend. People are introduced and there is a question and answer period.

- New members get a half day with the department head.

- Hold a special study session with the whole commission and city council (or board.)

- Each new commissioner has a one-on-one meeting, for one to two hours, with the City Manager.

Others you would like?

_____

_____

_____

_____

SKILLS OF A GOOD COMMISSIONER

You join a commission because you want to serve your community, use your unique skills, or advocate a particular interest. You soon learn the community-wide issues, and the political and interpersonal dynamics of both your commission and the community you serve. Commissioners wear different hats, requiring different skills at different times. However, every commissioner should have the following essential qualifications.

PERSONAL

- **Experience and maturity**; the emotional intelligence to manage the complexities of their role.

- **Openness** to new ideas; working with change and future prospects of the community require people with the imagination and flexibility to grasp and evaluate new ideas.

- **Altruism**; a desire to objectively serve the community with a broad-based view of the public interest.

- **Incorruptibility**; this means not only avoiding a mix-up of decision making and personal gain, but also avoiding the taking of sides on controversial issues on the basis of *who's* involved rather than *what's* at stake.

SUBSTANTIVE

- **Knowledge** of the process, objectives and laws. Commissioners should know the reasons for what they do, as well as the rules for doing it.

- **Interest** in activities and impacts beyond your own jurisdiction. No community is totally independent of what goes on beyond its boundaries, including what other agencies are doing nearby. Regional awareness matters.

PROCEDURAL

- **Awareness of your staff's** strengths, weaknesses and biases. Know the people advising you as unique human beings rather than information generators.

- **Distinguish between fact and opinion.** This is a primary skill for taking testimony at public hearings.

- **Express yourself clearly** in public. Thinking on your feet is probably not a skill you were taught in school. Take your time, take a deep breath, don't say too much, ask questions and engage others *(Page 47)*.

- **Take time** to prepare properly for meetings; planning is hard enough without having to play catch-up at the meeting. People who shoot from the hip usually miss the target.

Once a qualified commissioner takes a seat and goes to work, other skills are required. Some of the most important are:

- **Defining what's at issue** on any matter requiring a decision. It's vital to know beforehand what it is you have to decide—what is the main issue—the headline. Sometimes the first problem is deciding (or realizing) who, or what agency, has the problem. Ask, "Who's actually suffering financially, physically or psychologically?" If no one's suffering (or anticipates a large gain) where's the motivation to move ahead?

- **Assembling information** from both written and oral testimony and making meaningful recommendations to the people you advise. The recommendations should relate to adopted policies and plans, more than to your personal values.

- **Taking the initiative** in policy issues. Commissioners should be able to do more for their communities than react to what's placed before them on the agenda. If you're not equipped to give answers, a good commissioner will stop the permit or decision machine until answers are found.

- **Keeping the long view.** A good commissioner will develop a sense of how things done now will affect the future of the community, especially the welfare of people who aren't here yet—those special constituents of the planning process who are not in the room.

COMMISSIONER-STAFF RELATIONS

The quality of the relationship between the commission and staff influences the effectiveness of both. Ideally you have an open, trusting, comfortable, professional relationship.

Commissioners may want to more actively affect the department they watch over. More than just dealing with immediate issues presented by the staff, a commissioner might want to direct their own work and the future of the department; i.e. being passive, not proactive.

Staff members are often apprehensive of commissioners. Some feel that an active commissioner will interfere in their work, try to give assignments to staff, or make a nuisance of themselves. But a commissioner has very little authority. Only the commission acting as a group has authority.

What does an "active" commissioner do? Some commissioners suggest these actions, though you may not agree with them all. Check (✔) any that you'd like to discuss with your fellow commissioners.

___ 1. Gets involved in more than just the issues that staff presents.

___ 2. Asks staff to present their work plan for the year for your review, then each quarter for progress reports.

___ 3. Clarifies the different roles and responsibilities of staff and commission. (The town attorney might help here.)

___ 4. Requires written policies on recurring issues.

___ 5. Learns more about the field. (Asks staff for help on this.)

___ 6. Makes friends with staff. Has dinner with them before the meetings or meets afterwards. Gets to know the assistants.

___ 7. Is careful not to step outside your appropriate role, but uses this role positively and actively. Is careful when interjecting a personal opinion.

___ 8. Lets staff know that their work will be examined carefully.

___ 9. Brings in other community views.

___ 10. Reads the agenda package before the meeting.

___ 11. Discusses issues with other commissioners outside the formal meeting.

___ 12. Doesn't always react to the crowd; doesn't worry too much about offending people.

___ 13. Brainstorms ideas with the commission.

WHAT TO EXPECT FROM A GOOD COMMISSION(ER)

Every commission, board or council has obligations toward its staff. Here are a few. Which do your commission do well?

___ 1. We appreciate and publicly recognize and thank staff.

___ 2. We encourage professionals on the staff to use their judgment in stating views on professional matters, even if they are contrary to official policy.

___ 3. We understand and use a good decision-making process.

___ 4. We don't use staff members as scapegoats in political disputes. A commission or council should not hide behind its staff to avoid the heat from an unpopular decision.

___ 5. We help staff get to know the community. Facts can be discovered, but local values need to be understood as early as possible. Here the commissioners or council members can play the role of teacher.

___ 6. We work with staff through the director and don't bypass him or her to go directly to other members of the department for information or services—because this undermines the operation and organization of the department or agency.

___ 7. We work with their staff on the basis of confidence, openness, trust and goodwill.

___ 8. We don't use professional staff as office "gophers." While the functions of "going for coffee and donuts," etc., are important functions in any group, they are not appropriate functions for your professional staff. Similarly, you should not use your professional staff to develop meeting agendas alone, run commission meetings (except in certain specified situations) or take commission meeting minutes.

Others? _____

WHAT TO EXPECT FROM A GOOD STAFF

Staff provide the source and background for most commission, council and board decisions. This includes such topics as: What does the commission have to decide? What are the issues? What are the options and impacts of each? What is the staff's point of view and why? If the issue is significant, can the staff tie it back to broader policies and principles, or simply check it to see if it legally complies? See *Commission Summary Report (Page 55).*

Commissioners say that these areas are important. How is your staff's performance? Check (✓) those actions that your staff do well.

__ 1. They help the commission develop the basic facts necessary with clear, concise reports and well-organized long reports.

__ 2. They know what they are doing—the theory, principles, and process—and they can explain it to lay persons. They have a solid knowledge of the federal, state and local regulations governing their work and a current understanding of how to implement mandates.

__ 3. They work well with the public, applicants, other departments, special interest groups and other agencies. They don't embarrass commissioners in meetings.

__ 4. They know where and how to find necessary information for commission or council work.

__ 5. They keep current and stave off obsolescence.

__ 6. They communicate effectively and clearly, both orally and in written reports. They use graphics effectively in presentations. They write simply, clearly and non-bureaucratically, and use the active voice.

__ 7. They organize their time and work effectively. They meet realistic deadlines with finished work.

__ 8. They understand and use the four steps of the decision-making process *(Page 46).*

GET CONTROL OF THE AGENDA PACKAGE

Does your commission have control over the agenda package? If not, the chairperson can meet with the executive director of the staff and discuss this. Some staff might not want the commission to have more control (if they see it as interference), so tread carefully and always look for ways in which more order might help the director and staff do their own work. Here are some commissioner's suggestions.

1. With the director, review the purposes of the agenda package—both hers and yours.

2. Write down mutual goals, including what you'd each like to improve about the agenda package and hearing process.

3. Write down what you expect will be in each package.

4. Agree on the length and format for the *Summary Report (Page 55).*

5. Before each commission hearing, meet privately with the director for at least thirty minutes to review the agenda. Discuss HOW each item will be handled and what storm clouds may be brewing. Agree on what your minimum expectations are for the meeting *(Page 51).*

6. After each hearing, when the public has left, review informally with the staff and director how everyone is progressing on meeting your mutual goals to better manage the agenda package and meeting process.

7. Consider whether a *Public-Information Pamphlet (Page 54)* or a *Commissioner Handbook (Page 94)* might bring more order to the procedure.

Others?

_____

_____

REDUCE ROLE CONFLICTS

RESPONSIBILITY CHARTING

To deal with rapid change, some organizations focus on **understanding and resolving the conflicts between roles,** rather than defining roles in a hierarchical or pyramidal bureaucracy. They do this not by defining areas of jurisdiction, but by **defining roles and responsibilities in decision making** and conflict resolution.

To prepare a responsibility chart *(Page 34-35)* for your Commission, first write down the specific areas where decisions are made. Keep the list short. List these decision or work areas on the left. Across the top, name the decision makers (the people or office) connected with the work, department, project, section, etc.

Show the level of participation by any set of words that work for you; e.g., **R**esponsible for a particular decision (**R**); has the authority to **D**ecide (**D**); not responsible but must **A**pprove any decision made (**A**); need not approve but must be **C**onsulted (**C**); need not be consulted but should be **I**nformed (**I**), etc. Or you could simply note the level of authority; 1=high, 2=medium, 3=low.

To use the chart, the participants first identify and agree on major decision areas. Then each person (or group member) listed fills out the form privately. The results are aggregated and presented to the group. Individual responses are not identified.

Usually this shows wide variance in people's assumptions on who is responsible for what. The remainder of the meeting focuses on clarifying or aligning these differences. Dual responsibilities can be built in if needed, or expanded to avoid overlap—unless people want overlap.

The result is an agreement by all participants. It can be more useful than organization charts and job descriptions. Conflicts are visible and resolved to the extent possible. A follow-up meeting should be scheduled for three to six months out, to share how the chart has worked and to make changes.

MEMBERS includes anyone or any group having some authority or influence on, or who is affected by, actions in a **WORK AREA or ISSUE.**

Members might be: Commission, Chairperson, Staff, Project Manager, Department Director, Mayor, Town Council, Public, etc.

RESPONSIBILITY CHART

WORK AREA or ISSUE	M E M B E R S						
	Mayor/Town Council	Department Director	Chairman	Commission	Project Manager	Staff or Personnel	Public
Change in Budget	D	R					
Allocate Manpower		D	I				
Initiate Task Force	I	D	V	D			
Change Commission Agenda		R	D	V	C		I
Change Priorities/Goals	D	R					
Change Schedule/Work Progress	I	R				I	I
Enforce Regulations		R				I	I
Hear Appeals				R			
Manage Commission Meetings			R	A			
Mediate Commission-Staff Issues		R	C	C		I	

Level of Participation. Change these to suit your own situation.

R=**R**esponsible for **D**=**D**ecision authority **A**=must **A**pprove
I=should be **I**nformed **V**=can **V**ote **C**=should be **C**onsulted

*NB: The work areas, members and participation levels in the above
example are hypothetical, not real suggestions.*

On the next page is a blank Responsibility Chart. If
your commission has some confusing work areas or issues,
where you don't understand the lines of authority or responsibility, jot them down along with the main players (members) and fill in your best guess on the authority levels. Share
and discuss this with other commissioners.

YOUR RESPONSIBILITY CHART

M E M B E R S

NAME OF ORGANIZATION

_____

WORK AREA or ISSUE

R=**R**esponsible for   **D**=**D**ecision authority   **A**=must **A**pprove
I=should be **I**nformed   **V**=can **V**ote   **C**=should be **C**onsulted
Rename these categories to suit your own situation.

Section **3**

MANAGING MEETINGS

WHY DO WE HAVE COMMISSIONS AND PUBLIC MEETINGS?

"Commissioners" listed these reasons for public meetings.

1. For community input—a forum for public participation in society's decisions.

2. To inform people, to make citizens aware, to build community.

3. To advise elected officials and to enlarge the elected officials' decision powers.

4. To develop expertise in a specific area.

5. To explore issues, gather information, and exchange ideas, opinions and facts.

6. To resolve issues, develop a consensus or make a decision.

7. To gather evidence of the public need or support for something.

8. To meet state and local statutes, or meet a legal requirement.

9. To take the pressure (heat) off elected officials.

10. To guide and control government bureaucracies.

11. (Yours?)_____

_____

BALANCING THE COMMISSION MEETING CULTURE

Your commission meeting is a working culture. All cultures have two parts, the operational and the human. The key to productive commission meetings, with minimal conflict and effective outcomes, is balancing these two halves, balancing **what** you do with **how** you do it *(Page 17)*.

The bottom or operational half contains the meat, the plans, the applications, decisions, laws, procedures, etc. The top or human half contains how you do your business—particularly the values you show, such as openness, trust, involvement, listening, empathy and respect.

Commissions spend most time on the operational half. But too many largely ignore the top half. The result might be efficiency, but not community satisfaction and trust.

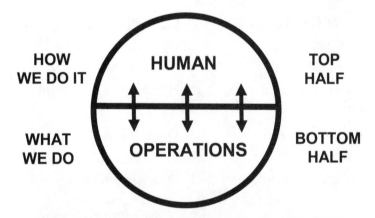

HOW
WE DO IT

HUMAN

TOP
HALF

WHAT
WE DO

OPERATIONS

BOTTOM
HALF

THE BALANCED WORK CULTURE

People's attitudes are more affected by **how** things are done than by **what** is done. Most of **what** commissioners do comes from outside their control: from applicants, staff, regulations and laws. In contrast, commissioners can mostly control **how** they do things.

People usually accept decisions if they are involved in them. If people don't feel involved, they may resist.

ADVERSARIAL AND CONSENSUS DECISIONS

There are two ways to reach a decision as a board, council or commission. Public groups typically use the adversarial or legal mode where opposing forces argue their case in front of the judicial body using Robert's Rules of Order *(Page 96)*.

This adversarial model works fairly well for simple issues, but poorly for the complex issues that commissions often face. For complex issues the consensus model is more effective.

A consensus position is one that everybody understands and is prepared to accept and support. It does not necessarily mean that everybody is keenly in favor of it, but it does mean that nobody is strongly opposed to it, or will undermine it later.

ADVERSARIAL	CONSENSUS
Us versus Them	We
Win-Lose	Win-Win
Focuses on differences.	Focuses on commonalities
Disagree	Agree
Enemy-Opponent	Friend-Person
Exclusive	Inclusive
Democratic voting	Dialogue and understanding
Positions are stated	Positions are heard No one strongly disagrees
Begins and ends at Step 4 of the decision process; i.e., argues positions *(Page 46)*	Systematically works through each of the four steps of the decision process
Litigation-Mediation	Consensus
Has a substantive position	Has no substantive position
May give or take ground	Establishes common ground
Majority is decided by vote	Consensus is arrived at and announced

THE COMMISSION'S PRODUCTS

Commissions and boards have two primary products:

DECISIONS and RECOMMENDATIONS

This is the overall commission procedure.

INPUT ⇨ | **PROCESS** | ⇨ **OUTCOMES** ⇨ **IMPACTS**

| People and Information | Commission Meeting | Decisions and Recommend-ations | On the Outside World |

Now let's look at how you like to make decisions—namely, your personal decision-making style.

YOUR DECISION-MAKING
AND PROBLEM-SOLVING STYLE—1

This quick inventory will help you see what parts of decision making you like best and where your conflicts could happen.

Picture yourself at a commission or board meeting, considering a problem or making a decision. Imagine what you are thinking and what you really do.

Below are eight horizontal rows of words arranged in four vertical columns. **Look at only one horizontal row at a time—e.g., the first row is:**

__ open   __ tentative   __ rational   __ practical

Write a 4 next to the word which best describes you when you are making a decision or considering a problem. Put a 3 alongside the word that fits you next best, a 2 against the word next most like you and a 1 next to the word least like you.

There are no preferred answers. The results will only be useful if you say how you actually are as a commissioner.

Number each word in each horizontal row; no blanks, no ties. Complete one full row at a time. **You are ranking across, not down.**

__ open	__ tentative	__ rational	__ practical
__ receptive	__ reserved	__ analytical	__ driving
__ feeling	__ watching	__ thinking	__ doing
__ accepting	__ observing	__ evaluative	__ constructive
__ involved	__ careful	__ logical	__ responsible
__ intuitive	__ perceptive	__ reasonable	__ active
__ present focused	__ reflective	__ future focused	__ pragmatic
__ experiencing	__ questioning	__ conceptualizing	__ experimenting

___ Total Col. 1   ___ Total Col. 2   ___ Total Col. 3   ___ Total Col. 4

Total each column. Read the next page.

YOUR DECISION-MAKING AND PROBLEM-SOLVING STYLE—2

Your four numbers suggest the weight you place on each of the four steps of the decision-making process, where you prefer to spend your time, i.e., the steps you find most interesting.

DO THESE WORDS SOUND FAMILIAR?

When members of your commission have a strong preference in one of these four areas of decision making, they might say things like those listed below. If you have a different decision style, you might be frustrated by what other commissioners say.

For example, if you like doing things right the first time, you'll probably feel frustrated if someone says, "Let's move on—we can fix any problems later."

1. Sense
"What actually happened?"
"Is that practical?"
"It worked last time."

2. Observe
"Do you have all the facts?"
"Let's think before leaping."
"Let's do it right."

3. Think
"I don't care if it doesn't work yet."
"It should work like this."
"What's the principle here?"

4. Act
"Let's get on with it."
"Let's stop talking about it."
"We can fix any problems later."

Now let's see how these different parts of decision making come together as the Commission Decision Process.

THE COMMISSION DECISION PROCESS

Healthy problem solving or decision-making processes usually follow a protocol similar to the one below. It is the scientific method, the process of logic.

1. ## SITUATION
   THERE IS A CONCRETE EVENT
   SOMETHING HAPPENS
   "WHAT'S THE PROBLEM?"

   There is information or some facts.
   An application is filed.
   Someone complains.
   A question is asked about a new issue.
   Data is collected.
   The affected groups and agencies are identified and invited.
   There is an analysis of what is wanted or what happened.
   The problem is described.

2. ## POSSIBILITIES
   THE ALTERNATIVES ARE EXPLORED.
   "WHAT COULD BE DONE?"

   What are the possibilities?
   What does the public say?
   What do they (staff, public, council, we) want?
   Commissioners make suggestions.

3. ## CRITERIA
   "HOW SHOULD WE CHOOSE?"

   Criteria are listed to help analyze and evaluate the alternatives; e.g., costs, benefits, impacts, timing, legality, policies and politics.
   The best alternatives become clear.

4. <u>ACTION</u>
A DECISION IS MADE
"WHO WILL DO WHAT?"

There is a recommendation to deny or approve.

There is a recommendation made to the staff or council.

There is a new commission policy for the area.

There is a decision to follow through and monitor.

_____

_____

4-STEP DECISION PROCESS

1
Situation?
What is the
Issue or
Problem?

2
Possibilities?
What are the
Alternatives?

Action?
What will
we do?
4

Criteria?
How should
we choose?
3

4-Step Decision Process

Questions:

Do your commission and your staff usually follow a similar process of problem solving?

Yes _____ No _____

If they did follow such a procedure, would it speed meetings, simplify the analysis of problems, and better organize the presentation of materials?

Yes _____ No _____

See page 101 for another version of this decision process that you could also use at public meetings.

MANAGING COMMISSION MEETINGS THROUGH QUESTIONS

The commission chair's job is building a strong problem-solving team, public trust, engagement and consensus. You can achieve this by asking questions of commissioners, staff or members of the public, following the 4-Step Decision Process.

THESE SUBSTANTIVE STATEMENTS CLOSE OUT PARTICIPATION	THESE OPEN, "PROCESS QUESTIONS" BUILD INVOLVEMENT AND COMMITMENT

1. To get at Issues, Facts or Problems:

These are the facts/issues.	What are the facts or issues here?
Here's the problem.	What's really the problem?
Here's what I think.	(Silence. They talk, you listen.)
This is our policy.	How does this fit with our policy?
These are the points.	What's involved here?

2. Looking for Alternatives/Possibilities:

Here's what I'd do.	What do you think we could do?
These are our choices.	What are the possibilities?
I think we should . . .	Let's spin around on this. Anyone?

3. Evaluating:

This is the best idea.	How should we judge the ideas?
It will cost too much.	How about costs?
These are the constraints.	What are the constraints on this?

4. Selecting, Deciding, Doing:

I want you to do this.	Who wants to pick up on this one?
I'm going to.	What should we do now?
Let me summarize.	What did we just agree to?
Here's the next step.	What's our (your) next step?

And the killer of them all. (Is this why you are short of time?)

I'll get back to you on this.	Let's set a time for you to bring us up to date with your work on this.

POWER, POLITICS AND MONEY

The higher you rise in government, the more that power, politics and money influence decisions. State and Federal legislation's stated goals often obscure major beneficiaries.

For example, a state legislator introduces a bill removing town and county regulations that restrict high-density development close to transportation centers. He promotes the bill as encouraging "accessible" housing and reducing greenhouse gas emissions (possibly by reducing driven miles).

What's Not Said?

A quick online search shows that in the last year this legislator received one half million dollars, 20% of his total campaign contributions, from the construction and real estate industry.

He may care deeply about the housing plight of the middle class and about greenhouse gas emissions, but he'd be ingenuous to not state how the legislation directly benefits his donors.

The public's trust in government is below 20%, a near all-time low. We trust people who speak the truth and do what they promise, qualities sorely missing in some elected leaders.

Our Representative Republic

We live in a mercantile democracy where business interests and money are active political participants. In our representative republic we elect leaders to (hopefully) promote our personal interests. We expect our elected representatives to "argue to win" *(Page 84)* for our side, for our interests, for our tribe. Public decisions are largely ruled by ideological and political interest group dynamics.

On this political stage—dominated by money, ideology and power—participation in public hearings is often window-dressing to largely predetermined votes. If you have ever spoken before a board or commission during the public comment section of decisions, you have likely experienced the irrelevance of what you said—like talking into a pillow. You might have even felt used and humiliated.

Honestly Describe the Situation

Step 1 of the 4-Step Decision Process *(Page 46)* asks, "What is the situation?" If you and your commission value transparency and honesty, do you really describe the full situation if you omit "political" information?

Claire Conner's (fictional) Sierra Meadows Planning Commission *(Page 1)* asked themselves, "Should we side with the traditional 'argue-to-win' cultural norm, where concealment, obfuscation and denial are optimal strategies—or should we adopt 'argue-to-learn', requiring honesty, openness and transparency?"

It takes money to run for public office. At the average town or county level it costs hundreds to thousands of dollars. A state-level campaign costs several million dollars. Even if some candidates fill much of their war chest with small individual contributions, almost all accept large donations from individuals, interest groups, corporations and PACs.

There is no sin in accepting money to get elected. It's the American way. The problem comes when elected officials pretend they are not influenced by these contributions. Contributors would need a lobotomy to separate their contribution from an anticipated benefit. Money, ideology and influence go hand-in-hand. Should you openly acknowledge that in your commission's decision process?

The first step in the 4-Step Decision Process is, "What's the situation? What's the problem?" With some issues, part of that situation is what's represented by a financial contribution and its related ideology. Politics is as important as (maybe more so than?) "scientific data" on environmental, traffic, or school impacts. It's nothing to be coy about. Political influence needs no more defensiveness or emphasis than a traffic study.

How legitimate is a description of the situation if it excludes a significant item? Attempts to be this objective may rattle some cultural norms. People may object that you shouldn't talk publicly about money and politics. They may become emotional, using inflammatory words like "corruption," "backroom dealings," or "exposé." But for the Sierra Meadows Planning Commission, money and politics are naturally included when describing a situation. They concluded that omitting it is dishonest.

You may disagree with their reasoning. It's a complex and potentially divisive subject. For them it was about values. "How do you want to live your life? What kind of a community do you want? How do you show that as a commission?"

DECIDE ON THE MEETING PURPOSE— THE PRODUCTS

You should be clear to yourself why the meeting is being held and what you expect from it. Here are some reasons:

- There is a pressing issue, application or permit needing resolution, a decision, or an answer.
- You want information or advice regarding an issue.
- You have a problem or concern and you want the group's ideas.
- Your peers or staff want the meeting.
- You want to announce something to everyone and get their reaction. You want to explain something.

It is usually not a good idea to hold a public meeting to:

- Deal with a personnel issue like hiring, firing, etc.
- Say something that can be said in a memo or by phone.
- Deal with a trivial subject.
- Deal with people who are hostile and angry.
- Deal with confidential material.

Come Prepared

- Know what you expect from the meeting.
- Let peers and staff know what you want from the meeting.
- Whenever possible, get agenda ideas from members before the meeting.
- Tell the group which of the four steps of the 4-Step Decision Process *(Page 46)* you want to cover on your agenda items.
- If you have already made up your mind firmly on a subject, let the group know.
- If appropriate, prepare a Summary Report *(Page 55)*.

When Leading the Meeting, Say Where You Are. Make sure everyone knows which step of the 4-Step Decision Process you are in. Your role as meeting leader is different at each step. *(See also Page 77.)*

Step 1. IDENTIFY OR DEFINE A PROBLEM.

There are three choices:

1. You tell them what the problem is as you see it; or
2. You ask them how each of them sees it; or
3. Both of these: i.e., you say your view and ask for theirs.

Note: If you tell fellow commissioners or staff what you think:

1) They might not say what they think, so you'll miss information they have that might be valuable in solving the problem; or

2) They might not agree with you and then see you as the opposition—not as the neutral chair. On the other hand, if you don't say what you think, they might simply wait for you to speak up or try to second-guess you. So what's best to do?

As the chair, you should say what you think only after the others have spoken, and only if no one said what you were thinking. When you give your opinion, make sure you don't use your authority to give your opinion more weight than theirs (or next time fewer will speak out and then all of you will be losers). *(Pages 64–67)*

Step 2. IDENTIFY THE POSSIBLE ACTIONS.

All ideas should be listed without comment or evaluation. Say, "We are in Step 2 (point to it): a neutral, uncritical listing of possible ideas and alternatives."

Step 3. EVALUATE THE POSSIBLE ACTIONS.

You ask commissioners and/or staff what they see as constraints reducing the number of ideas in Step 2. These might include existing policy, politics, cost, timing, laws, regulations, authority, technology, etc. The object here is not to criticize or evaluate the specific ideas listed in Step 2 but instead, to list factors helping everyone sort out which possible actions you can or should do something about, or which might be more acceptable.

It is particularly important for you not to criticize an idea, nor to be defensive, if someone evaluates one of your ideas. In all cases, you should be sure that you find out why others consider an idea unworkable; i.e., what their criteria are.

Step 4. DECIDE WHAT TO DO AND WHO WILL DO IT.

In this step, you apply the criteria of Step 3 to the ideas of Step 2. Don't make a detailed one-on-one comparison. Just look at each list side by side. Often it will be a simple process; what to do is obvious, staring everyone in the face.

You might say, "Please look at what you have said on the problem, the options and the selection criteria. What does this suggest?" Let them decide what seems to be the best solution. A consensus guarantees a good solution and assures the group's commitment to making their chosen solution work.

Finally, recap what was agreed on, who will do what and when they will do it. To be extra clear on next steps, follow through and staff actions, write everything down publicly during the meeting so everyone can see it on the overhead TV screen.

COMMISSION PUBLIC-INFORMATION PAMPHLET

Your commission meetings will be shorter and more effective if you develop a brief information sheet or pamphlet and leave a stack by the door. This pamphlet can be a simple 8½" x 11" or 8½" x 14" three-fold including:

1. The name of the commission.

2. Names (plus optional address and phone number) of each commissioner and the department manager (or city manager, county executive, or executive director).

3. A brief summary of the authority of the commission, what it controls and who it reports to. What the commission can and can't do. What is the difference between staff and commission? Who has final authority over what?

4. A statement of the overall mission or purpose of the commission, what it plans to achieve during the next year and how it plans to do it.

5. Key decisions made over the last year or two that might interest the public.

6. The basic meeting Agenda, including the sequence of events for hearings, rules for public input, rebuttals, etc. This is the framework the chairperson uses to manage the meeting.

7. Dates and locations of meetings and a phone number for more detailed information.

8. The appeal procedure.

9. Other folders or information papers available on request.

10. How people can best use the commission, including how to use you as a partner (and not see you as an obstruction or adversary).

Keep it brief and simple. If it becomes a big task to prepare this pamphlet, then it is being done incorrectly. Developing this pamphlet may improve commission and staff relations. The full commission reviews the draft copy before printing.

COMMISSION SUMMARY REPORT

On all major issues coming before the commission, the staff analysis should include a one-page Summary Report.

At commission meetings, this summary is valuable public information. Be sure to have enough copies for everyone. It complements the *Commission Public-Information Pamphlet (Page 54)*. Together they form the foundation for managing public discussion *(Page 77)*. The report gives the following information listed as a series of one-liners:

A. **Project identification** information, including names of applicants.

B. The **problem** or request as first presented, plus all the **key issues** or problems later identified. "What is the problem/issue/situation?" (Decision Process Step 1, *Page 46*.)

C. The major **alternatives** or possibilities. "What could we do?" (Step 2.)

D. The major **criteria** to help rank or choose between alternatives. "How should we choose?" (Step 3.)

E. The **staff recommendation** (if any). (Part of Step 4.)

F. The **options** available to the commission or board, e.g.:
- **Approve.**
- Approve with **modifications.**
- **Disapprove** or deny.
- **Put over** until a following meeting.
- **Refer** to another commission or to council.

MANAGING MEETING TIME

Many commissions spend too much time on their meetings. Here are some typical time-related problems reported by commissioners. Do you have any of these? Check (✓) the ones that apply:

___ 1. The hearings are too long.

___ 2. We don't follow any regular procedure.

___ 3. Commission members seem to ask the same questions over and over.

___ 4. Public testimony gets repetitive.

___ 5. We don't deal with hostility or conflict very well.

___ 6. There is too much material to go over beforehand and at the hearing. "Revising past minutes in public is ridiculous."

___ 7. Decisions are made too easily or too quickly.

___ 8. Voting on certain issues is too predictable.

___ 9. We put simple, "automatic approval" items first on the agenda. The public sees their important items far down or last and believes we are manipulating them. We don't explain this.

Here are some suggestions for managing time problems.

1. **MANUAL:** Develop a procedural manual and stick to it regarding how you handle topics and issues. See *Public-Information Pamphlet, (Page 54)*.

2. **TIME:** If you don't yet use the 4-Step Decision Process *(Pages 46 and 77)*, then set fixed time boundaries on both the overall meeting and on individual presentations. Announce an overall time for the pro-X group (say, 1/2 hour) and the same time for the anti-X people. Then say, "Individual speeches will be limited to a maximum of two (or three) minutes." Stick to it. If a presenter gets repetitive, ask him to introduce **only** new material, not points already covered. Write issue topics on the overhead. Use

a clock, buzzer, or light visible to all *(Page 77)*.

Feel free to interrupt a speaker: "Yes, you are making an interesting point, but the current area of discussion is XYZ. Can you tell us how your statement relates to that?" or, "Yes, I hear you are speaking to the ABC point to which others have already spoken. Do you have something new to add? In the interest of time, we are asking people to limit their discussion only to **new** points. Is that OK with you?" Writing what they said—showing you are listening—helps people accept this.

Feel free to guide and control the framework of the hearing. If a person is wandering off the question, interrupt them and restate the question. When you reach the rebuttal stage, stop any new information. Introduce the rebuttal step by stating what the points are so far, and limit rebuttal to just these points.

3. **KNOW WHO IS THERE AND THE ISSUES:** Before the hearing, have members of the public fill out 3 x 5 cards with their name, their address (outsiders can take up time and influence the meeting's tone and perception), their view or area of interest, and if they want to speak before the commission. *(See also Page 77.)*

The chair uses these to sense the range of concerns and to plan the time needed for public presentations. Summarize the card issues, and the number of people for each issue, so everyone knows what's in the room.

If you are brave (or foolish?), you might say you realize that people who attend public meetings usually represent special interests—not always the general public—and as a commission, you must keep that in mind.

4. **LISTEN AND RESPOND:** Be clear to the public what you hear. Write single-line summaries of points on a laptop and overhead screen, whiteboard or pad, etc. Or nod your head and restate what they said in very brief terms. The reason for this is to show the audience that their points are being recognized, so they don't feel compelled to repeat them over and over and over and over and over.

After the public-input phase, the chair might ask each commissioner to briefly state any other main points that he or she heard. Don't allow discussion or evaluation at this step; just list points. This will give everyone a full picture of what the commissioners heard as important. Ideally, these should be written on the screen for all to see. At minimum, the chair should list the points on his or her notepad and restate them.

5. **INFORMATION FOR ALL**: Make sure everyone is well informed on the facts. Create a simple facts/information handout, in advance, for every public meeting on important or contentious items. Include physical and financial numbers, timelines, environmental/traffic/etc. impacts, issues, and affected groups/organizations, etc. See *Commission Summary Report (Page 55)*.

   Hostility and disagreement often happen when people lack information, or have different information or misinformation, or feel excluded. There should be very little new material presented at any hearing. Hearings are times for discussion, public opinions, etc.

6. **STAFF PREPARATION**: Staff should take pre-hearing materials and boil them down to their bare bones. The key issues should be listed as a series of one-sentence statements. This summary should preface each hearing package. If commissioners don't trust staff to do this objectively, hold an executive session and get the trust issue resolved *(Page 32)*.

7. **TRUST**: It is critical for the commissioners to trust the chair and his/her impartiality as a facilitator of the commission process. In light of this, the chair should rarely, if ever, state his or her opinion on content, only on procedure. To state a content-related view will only weaken the chair as the facilitator of the commission's hearing process.

   This role may not be acceptable to a chair who wants to use the power of the position to influence a decision's content; however, this is a questionable use of the chair.

If a chair wishes to present his or her personal content position, he might consider telling the audience he is aware that what he is doing is out of keeping with his role; e.g., "If it is acceptable to the commission, I would like to briefly take off my impartial hat as chair and state my personal views on this subject . . . Thank you. That's all I want to say. Now I'll resume my chair role." Some chairs step down from the podium to do this. [Yes, they really do!] *(Page 68)*

8. **CONTINUANCES**: Feel free to move for a continuance on items when insufficient information is available or if the public seems unusually divided or antagonistic. If you do move for a continuance, clearly explain why, what will be needed to successfully settle the issue, when you will resume the hearing (usually at the next meeting) and who is responsible for coordinating the parties and information for the commission. If you need to set up a special study session, do it. See *Task Force (Page 69)*.

9. **AUTHORITY**: Be clear to yourselves and to the public just what your authority is. Be clear who has the problem; i.e., who suffers financially, physically or psychologically? Those affected must be present for a consensus decision.

   Have a single-sheet *Public-Information Pamphlet (Page 54)*, stating your mission, goals, authority, etc. This should be available for everyone at every hearing. The commission hearing procedure is in that pamphlet, which enables the chair to remind the public exactly what step the hearing is at, and what is and is not appropriate at that step.

10. **STRATEGIC PLAN**: Developing an overall strategic plan with the Executive Director and staff directs and aligns energies of the commission and staff toward the same goals, rather than into conflicting or insignificant areas.

Notes:

SEVENTEEN STEPS TO BETTER MEETINGS

Highlight (✔) any of the following actions you'd like to try at your public meetings. You probably won't use many of these at informal meetings.

BEFORE THE MEETING—PREPARE

1. **Plan**, along with the staff, who should be there, what do you want to achieve, how much public participation do you want? Will this be a decision-making meeting?

2. Send out the **agenda** and information sheets ahead of the meeting. People should have as much advance information as possible, so they can thoughtfully prepare their response and comments. See also *Commission Summary Report (Page 55)*.

3. Come early to **set up the room**. Have the materials you need: pads, whiteboard, markers, laptop, TV overhead.

AT THE BEGINNING OF THE MEETING

4. **Start on time**. Introduce people if necessary. If you want public participation, people should feel comfortable. Provide coffee, tea, or soft drinks at small, long meetings.

5. **State the agenda**, your role, the public's role, the time limit and what you want to achieve during that time. Revise these if necessary.

6. **Start with action items** carried over from the last meeting. At a more formal meeting, adopt the last meeting's minutes.

DURING THE MEETING

7. Use a **standard method** for handling recurring types of problems. You might always refer items in a certain area to one person, or you might ask whose area the problem is in, or you might always poll the group for where to begin, or on what the issue really is.

8. **Watch yourself.** Meeting leaders often get nervous, talking when they should be silent or pushing when they shouldn't. If you feel anxious or defensive, relax, stop

talking, take a deep breath, sip some water and look around.

9. **Summarize** what people say on the overhead TV, white-board, or easel pad, asking if you heard each item correctly. Invite comments, use questions, use silence, remind people of the agenda topic. If you answer a question, check with the person who asked it: "Did we answer your question?" *(Page 47).*

10. If you are using a consensus decision process, such as the one recommended in this book, **control off-topic comments**. Remind people of which step in the process you are at. Put up the 4-Step Decision Process *(Page 46 and 101),* and point to the current step.

AT THE END OF THE MEETING

11. Read aloud the agreed-on **action items**: who, what, when.

12. Set the date, time and place for the **next meeting**.

13. **Evaluate** the meeting (how well it went today). *(Page 62)*

14. **Close** the meeting on time and on a positive note. Thank everyone for attending and participating.

AFTER THE MEETING

15. **Clean up** the room (think of the next user).

16. Send out the **meeting minutes**, or a memorandum of understanding if appropriate.

17. **Follow up** on your action items.

Notes:

_____

_____

_____

_____

IMPROVE YOUR MEETINGS WITH CUSTOMER FEEDBACK

Having the public attend, then evaluate your meetings, gives you valuable feedback on your performance as a commission, board or council. When you use their suggestions, it tells citizens you value what they think, and that you are trying to do the right thing by them.

Written Evaluation

Leave a short evaluation form by the door. You could pass it out to everybody at the meeting. At the end of the meeting, and perhaps also during the meeting, ask attendees to complete the form and leave it in the labeled box. It is yours. Ask what you want to know. As your needs change, update the form. Here are some ideas:

Public Participation

Did you speak at today's meeting?   No ☐   Yes ☐
If yes, did the (name of your Commission) listen to and hear you?
No ☐   Not Sure ☐   Yes ☐

Decisions

Were you satisfied with the decision process used today?
No ☐   Not Sure ☐   Yes ☐
Were you satisfied with the final decision or outcome on your issue today?
No ☐   Not Sure ☐   Yes ☐

Comment or Suggestion:

_____

_____

Verbal Evaluation

At the end of the meeting, do a public "plus-delta". Use two columns. At the top of the left column, put + (plus). At the top of the right column, draw a triangle Δ (delta). Explain, *"The plus is what you liked about this meeting—things we should keep for next time. The Greek letter delta, which is the technical symbol for change, is what you would like to see done differently next time."*

For each column, invite one idea from each person. *"Please say one thing you liked about the meeting and one thing you'd like to see changed."*

Write what they say. Make no comment, except, *"Thank you."* Keep it brief.

The list is usually short. Many people say nothing. Commit to change what people want changed. Bringing the notes to the next meeting shows that you are following through.

How Was The Meeting?

+	**Δ**
Clear Agenda.	Some people rambled.
Liked information handout.	Invite Design Review.
Next step is clear.	Explain the decision process better.

Using feedback improves the quality of meetings, and it moves the meeting culture towards more trust, less conflict, more openness and better participation.

CHAIRPERSON'S ROLE IN FACILITATING A CONSENSUS

When you are chairing or leading a meeting or group and you want agreement on a problem or issue, keep in mind the following role. It focuses on common ground, avoids conflict and builds consensus.

1. **Accept all comments** at face value. Assume no side or covert meanings. Be simple, act naively and avoid judging or giving your opinion.

2. **Deny your authority** as a leader by passing authority back to the group. "Does anyone have any thoughts?" Hold the group accountable for its own actions. Ask the group to mediate its own internal squabbles. Reflect content questions back to the group for clarification or comment: e.g., "Would someone like to answer?" Otherwise, you stay silent.

3. Ask the **group to assess their progress** toward group goals. "How are we doing? Any ideas to help us work better?" Remind the group of their agreed-upon ground rules. Remember that your initial task as a leader is to help them agree on the meeting process ground rules; namely, how we will run the meeting *(Page 54).*

4. **Ground rules.** Ask those who don't agree on the rules, but want to stay in the meeting, to consider the validity of their position.

5. **Competence.** Turn outwardly focused expectations back into the group. If the person talks about "them out there," help him or her see that there is competence and responsibility in the room to do the job. If another group should be invited to the discussion, invite them.

6. **Authority.** Avoid suggesting that there is one best way, a hidden answer, or a solution known to you or to the department or commission. The answer is theirs—the group's.

7. **Group ideas.** Ask for suggestions from the group as a

whole, rather than from one person, "Does someone have an idea?" *(Page 47)*

8. **Check** if a suggestion offered by someone is acceptable to the person who voiced the concern or question: "Did we answer your question?"

9. **Intervene** when members disagree or raise objections to each other's ideas; e.g., "Before we start judging ideas, let's first hear from everyone on how they see . . . (restate the problem). We can evaluate later, OK?"

10. **Encourage** someone to explain a tentative or incomplete idea. Probe to see if there is a suggestion or concern behind a question; e.g., "Say some more." "What were you thinking?" "Did you have an idea of what we could do?" "Why?"

11. **Clarify understanding**—ask for confirmation of your understanding if someone is rambling; e.g., "And tell us how that connects to . . . (restate the topic)."

12. **Clarify subject**—inform someone that a topic is outside the framework of the discussion.

13. **Postpone**—ask someone to refrain from introducing a new topic until the current one is finished with; e.g., "That's a good point, but if it's OK with you, can we first finish discussing the one we are on and then get back to it?"

14. **Constructively criticize** to indicate that an idea is not acceptable—yet.

15. **Return**—get back to someone you had asked to wait to enter the discussion.

16. **Record**—make a visible, public note of what is said. If someone doesn't think they were heard, they'll probably turn up their volume or feel ignored (and later, may try to get even).

17. **Time boundary**—signal the group that you're about to end the discussion, and provide direction for the last few minutes.

Additional suggestions from some commissioners on what the chair should do:

- **Take responsibility** for the process.

- **Maintain a strong relationship** with the staff. Make sure everyone understands their job and role *(Page 32)*.

- **Develop a consensus** on who we are and where we are going.

Others?

_____

_____

_____

_____

_____

HOW DOES THE CHAIRPERSON INTRODUCE HIS OR HER OWN SUBSTANTIVE VIEWS?

Experienced leaders know they must be very careful when introducing their own substantive views into a discussion before the commission. Here's why.

In his memoirs, Napoleon tells this story: One evening, he sat outside his tent with his generals, planning the next day's battle. While discussing a certain battalion, he glanced at a nearby hill. On waking the next morning, he looked up and saw the battalion on the hill. When asked why it was there, a general replied, "Isn't that what you wanted, Sir? You looked at the hill last evening as we discussed that battalion."

Most leaders have experienced this. People like to please leaders—and hesitate to contradict them.

A key role of the chair—the commission leader—*(Page VI)*, is facilitating the commission decision process. A facilitator should be neutral; i.e., not be seen by another member as holding a position on the matter. Whenever the chair speaks out on a substantive (in contrast to a procedural) matter, there is sure to be at least one member of the commission or audience who has another position. That person no longer experiences the chair as the neutral facilitator but as an opponent.

When this happens, the chair has lost the power of leadership for that person or group. The chair should always try to maintain power so they can facilitate an objective, high-quality decision process that participants feel is fair.

This is a particularly difficult point for many commissioners or board members to accept. *"Why, for gosh sakes, I got on the commission because I had strong feelings on the subject."* or, *"They appointed me because I have a lot of expertise in this area. Now you tell me I should keep quiet, * * * * !"*

How do you introduce facts, information, or just plain opinions you have, while keeping yourself in the driver's seat as chairperson?

Some commissioners have suggested:

- Do it through staff beforehand.

- Step down from your role as chair and introduce the material in front of the commission as a citizen (this is very tricky and may not be accepted by some). *(Page 59)* [Yes, they really do!]

- Hold informal discussions on the subject, where you are free from the responsibilities of actual decision making.

- Keep your mouth closed until the end of the discussion. Perhaps someone else will bring up the same point. On the other hand, if no one does, perhaps the point wasn't so important after all.

If you feel you must introduce a substantive point, try it as a question. "Have we looked into the . . . area on this one?" or "What about the . . . ?" Note: if no one picks up the ball, it might be best to simply leave it.

Others?

_____

_____

_____

_____

_____

As the chair, remember it is better to lose the battle (your personal view or point) and win the war (your leadership ability to guide and manage the development of the commission and community). "Winning battles is for soldiers. Winning wars is for generals."

COMMISSION TASK FORCE OR SUB-COMMITTEE

A task force or sub-committee can quickly examine an acute problem or issue. It is a small team, authorized by the commission, representing all groups with a vested interest in the task force's results. Task forces expose members to the workings of the commission and staff, and provide citizens with the opportunity to effect change.

It should feel empowered and independent, free to ask questions and bounce ideas and problems off the commission and others. It should keep the commission informed on progress so that its final report has no surprises.

Suggest that task force members see themselves as representing the whole community or organization, not just their special interests or home department. Give the group a short time-line and a clear goal or definition of success.

PROCEDURE

A task force might use the 4-Step Decision Process *(Page 46)*:

1. **Define** their assigned **task** and **list the main issues** or problems.

2. **Brainstorm** and **list** what members see as **possible solutions** or actions that could be taken to solve the problem(s) listed.

3. Then **list the criteria** that members see as constraining the possible solutions; i.e., legal, financial, time, or other factors pointing to workable ideas from list 2 above.

4. **Write the recommendation**(s).

5. **Prepare and submit the task force report** to the commission. This report should briefly summarize the main items from Steps 1 through 4 above, so that the commission can understand the task force's decision process. A good report should rarely exceed six pages. The main points should be summarized on Page 1.

RECOMMENDATION

A recommendation from a task force to the commission will usually take one of two forms. It will be either **substantive** or **procedural,** though occasionally a report will be purely informational.

Substantive recommendations are specific solutions to the problem; e.g., "We recommend adoption of the following policy."

Procedural recommendations answer the question, "Where do we go from here," to further explore a complex or subtle problem; e.g.:

"We have listed the key issues and suggest that a task force explore the following areas (list them) in detail, and that the following people and organizations affected by this (list them) will be contacted for their input. This task should take four weeks or less." Or:

"We recommend that the issues as listed be circulated within these departments (list them), and written reactions and comments be brought to the commission before its next meeting."

When the task force's job is complete, it should disband.

FREQUENTLY ASKED COMMISSION QUESTIONS

The *Commission Summary Report (Page 55)* and the *Commission Public-Information Pamphlet (Page 54)* probably answer these and similar questions for most agenda items.

Questions that are asked regularly at commission meetings (from both the public and commissioners) include:

ARE YOU ALWAYS READY TO RESPOND?

1. Why weren't we notified sooner?
2. This is the first time I've seen the staff report!
3. How much time do we have?
4. How much will it cost?
5. Is it in the budget?
6. Do I have to sign in?
7. Why can't you leave things the way they are?
8. What are you outsiders doing here?
9. Isn't that what you're getting paid for?

Make sure you know the answers!

Other frequently asked questions from YOUR Commission meetings?

_____

_____

_____

Section **4**

WORKING WITH DIFFICULT PEOPLE

MANAGING THE EMOTIONAL SETTING

Set a physical and psychological stage that reduces conflict and hostility. Most people come to public meetings to support or oppose something. When they see you as an ally, inviting their participation and hearing what they say, they will be more trusting, and less inclined to flag-waving, posing and opposing.

The **emotional picture** to create for your commission meeting is a place where people feel welcomed and heard. Imagine a comfortable situation where you're enjoying a conversation: maybe sitting together on a sofa, or seated on either side of a small, round café table, or chatting by a watercooler.

The physical layout of a commission meeting room encourages—or discourages—dialog, participation and consensus building. Many commissions meet in the town council chambers, using the slightly raised dais, curved table and microphones. However, if the dais is too high, forcing citizens to look uncomfortably up at the commissioners, it discourages equality and good relationships.

As Claire Conner described *(Page 6)*, the Sierra Meadows Planning Commission set up a triangle, where public and commission focused on the overhead TV screen, rather than facing (confronting) each other.

Large meetings. Large cities and counties, or powerful state or regional commissions, can create a more participatory environment with a gently sloping floor, where the public looks down at the elected or appointed officials. That helps balance the inordinate power that appointed and elected officials present by sitting as a group, on the other side of a high wall—with all the trappings of authority and control including flags and insignia—a traditional physical arrangement encouraging compliance, but also resentment and hostility.

Increase Participation. If you truly want participation (and who these days thinks they can run government any other way?) you will state this very clearly by HOW you run the meeting. When you are open and clear about the meeting structure; describe its decision process, rules, content, purpose and outcomes; and summarize and record what people say, you show that you welcome participation.

Reduce Anxiety. Many people are apprehensive about speaking publicly. The chair should acknowledge anxiety, "I understand that speaking in a public situation like this is difficult for some, but we need your ideas and opinions. Without them we could not be a true community and would not be able to find the best solutions to the problems (situation, issues) that we face this evening. So please take your time. We are listening."

Repeat that regularly during the public-participation part of the meeting.

ACTIVE LISTENING TO GET RESULTS

Active listening is far more difficult than passive listening or telling. As an active listener, you focus on what is being said, integrate it into your past experience and knowledge, understand what is meant (the feelings, as well as the words), give feedback on what you heard—including your understanding of what the speaker said—and confirm that you understand what he or she meant.

A good way to show understanding and listening is paraphrasing back what was said: in other words, simply restate what you heard. This may take just one key word from the last sentence or several sentences on your part. If you truly did not understand what was said, just say so: for example, "You made a lot of points there, and I'm sorry but I missed your main point" or "Could you say some more?" or "I don't understand yet. Please try me again."

Improve communications by increasing the amount of information *(Pages 54–55)*. Lack of information leads to isolation and paranoia. That builds resistance, not cooperation. Get as much information out as possible and get it out early. This doesn't mean flooding people with all the details (unless they ask), but summarize the main facts, the key things they should know or the items that affect them.

What you think of as a "good job" may not be the same as what the Town Manager, Department Chief, or staff members think. Bring all these views together for your work as a commissioner to have lasting effect.

Remember that staff views tend to prevail in the long run—commissioners come and go. Building understanding and commitment from all affected parties is key to lasting agreements.

WORDS THAT WORK—BEYOND NIMBY

NIMBY means **N**ot **I**n **M**y **B**ack **Y**ard, a common public response to generalized fears that a proposed project will bring undesirable elements (people, activities, business, traffic, . . .) or depress property values. The 4-Step Decision Process *(Page 46)* helps people clarify their often-vague fears, and it eases their concerns that they are not being heard.

Reduce Conflict—Bring Order to Chaos

Public participation is messy, often confusing. For many attendees, this will be their first commission meeting. Many came because they have questions and concerns, often vague and general. It is the board or commission's responsibility to help everyone understand the range of concerns as well as the specific issues, and then to answer questions. For a legitimate decision process, all affected parties should be present.

Many attendee questions will be answered by the *Commission Summary Report (Page 55)* and the *Commission Public-Information Pamphlet (Page 54)*.

The commission member (usually the chair) opens the public input with Step 1 of the 4-Step Decision Process *(Page 46)*.

Who is Here?

"Thank you all for coming this evening. We will begin by understanding the range of issues and concerns present in the room. I'd like to know why you came today, by asking you four questions.

"The first question will be, "Who is here to generally support the proposal (issue, topic, plan, project, study, etc.)?" The second is, "Who is here to generally oppose the project?" The third will be, "Who is here to support the proposal if it is modified in some way?" The fourth is, "Who came just to get information about the issue?" Your answers are not a vote on the project. They will tell us who is in the room, so that we can have a more-informed discussion and meeting.

For and Against?

"Let me first ask who is here to generally support the proposal? Please raise your hand. Thank you." (You might roughly tally the number of hands and type it on the TV screen for all to see.) "Second, who is here to generally oppose the proposal, please raise your hand? Thank you." (Tally and type this number as before) "Third, who is here to maybe support the plan if it is modified in some way?" (Tally and type.) "Thank you. And finally, who is here mainly to get information or answers?" (Tally and type.) "Thank you all very much."

Issues, Concerns, Problems

"Now I'd like to help us all understand what specific concerns are present, particularly from those of you who are opposed to the project (proposal, plan, etc.) before us today.

"Sometimes people oppose a project because they don't want any development; they want things to stay as they are. Other people might be concerned for the project's potential effect on traffic, schools, property values or neighborhood character.

"To help us understand your range of concerns, I'll ask you to raise your hands when I say one of the issues or concerns we have already heard about this proposed project. You can see the list of issues on the overhead screen and in the *Summary Report (Page 55)*. But before we go around the room again, are there any additional issues, concerns, or problem areas you have that are *not* listed?" (If there are, add them.)

"Thank you. And please remember that if you are generally opposed to the project, we would like to know why—namely, what particular concern or issue lies behind your opposition.

"Let's begin with the first item on the list. How many of you are concerned about the effect of the project on traffic (or nuclear waste, or whatever the issues are)?" Go down the list, perhaps recording a tally of the numbers of people signaling their interest on each problem area.

"Thank you very much. This gives us all a much better sense of the concerns in this room.

Managing Time

"You have the meeting agenda, which shows the times allocated for each item. We will now begin the thirty-minute General Comments section.

"It is the published policy of this commission that each public comment is limited to three minutes. Can you see the clock? I will make a mark on the overhead next to the issue(s) you are addressing, so you'll know that we hear you.

"If I did not mark or note a point you are making, please let me know. It's important that the commission hear all the issues, and it is equally important that you know we are listening and hear you.

"Please begin by saying your name and address. We give priority to residents.

"Thank you."

Do you think **this process takes too much time**? Yes? Well the opposite is true! It cuts repetition, eliminates contentious arguing, and brings rapid agreement on high-quality, supported decisions. It's both effective and efficient.

TALKING

*"I talk and watch you listen as you watch me talking.
You talk and watch me listen as I watch you talk."*—Unknown

In any conversation a lot is happening beyond the words. Only 20% of communications is verbal. The remaining 80% is nonverbal (body language, eyes, unconscious past meanings, etc.).

Our talking is constantly and instantly modified by the way we see how the listener is hearing us. It's one of the tightest feedback loops we know.

Here are six common ways of communicating. When you are talking in your role as a commissioner, try to stay with the first three. They lead to understanding, communicating and learning. The last three move towards threatening, self-defeating, unsatisfying results.

a) **CREATIVE TRANSLATION**—Speculating about the meaning, the messages and the feelings of the other. "When you say that, is it because you believe . . . ?"

b) **TRUTH**—Revealing things about yourself, your beliefs, motivations and feelings. Saying why you are saying what you say.

c) **INQUIRY**—Listening, observing and asking questions *(Page 47)*. Trying to understand. "Please say some more." "Can you tell us what happened?"

a) **DECEPTION**—Incongruities between feelings and words. Saying one thing while believing something different. Fraud.

b) **ATTACK**—Value judgments: "That's wrong." Advice: "You should do this . . ." and Blaming: "You always . . ." or "It's your fault."

c) **SILENCE**—And other sullen, withdrawn behaviors.

Are your commission communications staying with the first three? Or...?

Between commissioners?

_____

_____

With the public at commission meetings?

_____

_____

With staff, town council, or related higher authority?

_____

_____

GOOD COMMUNICATIONS

In public meetings, communications often break down when the two parties have come to different conclusions about something they each care passionately about. In the pressures of the moment, groups often jump too quickly to conclusions and actions (e.g., Step 4 of the 4-Step Decision Process). Battles and resentments follow. That's bad for people and community. **Jumping too quickly to Step 4 is why we have so many lawyers per square foot in the USA!** *(Page 7)*

Some differences are real—people have different needs. But many conflicts can be avoided if people take time listening to how others see the problem—**before** discussing solutions.

80% of communications is nonverbal. Of the 20% that's verbal, about one-fifth is rational. The rest consists of emotions, voice tone, feelings, etc. Relying too much on logic can be fatal. When you smile honestly, you can say almost anything without provocation. Use every chance to make the other person feel comfortable and important.

Arguing is a poor tactic. Don't expect anyone to change their mind by being told or argued with. Remember, as far as the other person sees the situation, their position is correct. It is better to ask questions, to draw them out. Have others explain how they see the situation; how they see the problem. Sharing views and beliefs leads both parties to their common ground *(Page 15)*, and begins building consensus.

Control your desire to win. Pointing up weaknesses in another's position, while possibly honest, is escalation. It is better to back away from any conclusions or positions and seek common ground on mutual problems. Winning an argument often means losing the person. Don't argue to win. Argue to understand *(Page 84)*.

Manage disagreements early. Get to arguments when they appear. If someone complains, ask them to repeat it, "So I can be sure I understand." Repeating the complaint shrinks it. With disagreements, stay on the problem, not on personalities. If groups disagree, ask them to get together and work it out. If they can't, meet with them and help them work through the decision process together. Show them how much they both care about the issue. Mutual caring might be their first common ground.

There is no right answer. Most public issues are complicated—and often there is no one right answer. **If you want a good decision, use a good decision process.** Include the views of all the major players involved and affected. **Start with Step 1,** which explores "The Situation"—not with Step 4, which jumps too quickly to answers, positions, conclusions or solutions. Build consensus. Get everyone on board.

ARGUE TO WIN OR ARGUE TO LEARN?

Our fictional Sierra Meadows Planning Commission struggled internally with this question. Here is their thinking.

In a battle, your best strategy is withholding information and concealing your position. That's usual in a traditional adversarial public hearing processes—but are those good community values?

This commission believes that it shows real strength when it is open, truthful, understanding and empathetic to the wide range of personalities, values and interests in their community.

People who like fighting may call openness "weakness," but fighting contributes to the polarization and alienation we all experience today. As a commission, they didn't want to support that. They felt they could do better, as Sierra Meadows is their home, where their families live.

They quickly discovered that people who argue to win, who are closed and defensive, used the commission's openness to attack. The commission realized that people who like fights live in a stark, black-and-white, yes-and-no, right-and-wrong "zero-sum" world, where civil wars have one winner and one destroyed loser. These people use openness to hit commissioners hard.

The commissioners have been accused of being naïve, or wishy-washy, or both. For example, if one is personally attacked in a meeting and summarizes the attack on the overhead screen during Step 1 of the decision process *(Page 9)*, they appear, to some, like a wuss. *"Why don't you shout back, 'That's a load of crap—and it's irrelevant!'"*

If they are attacked at public meetings they don't cave. They stand calm and still, not pushing, but not falling back. The public then sees that the commission is honest, open and transparent, doing the right things and doing them right. This brings powerful community trust and support.

RESPONDING TO HOSTILE QUESTIONS

Recognize that the attack is not directed at you personally—so don't take it personally. Most hostility has little to do with the immediate situation.

It may come from home, from their past experience with authority, or from fear (e.g., losing property value), whether justified or not. See it as one way that a person expresses his or her frustrations and anxieties.

As a commissioner, if you argue, defend or fight back, you have escalated the battle and lost your role. Your role is to maintain an environment where work is done, building understanding and effectively resolving community issues. Don't escalate; don't join the fight.

There are several ways to respond to hostility; some are productive and some are not. You can:

a) **ENGAGE DIRECTLY**—Fight back, escalate, and join the battle.

b) **ENGAGE INDIRECTLY**—Wait until later and shove. "Don't get mad; get even."

c) **WITHDRAW**—You "leave the room" emotionally; back off; stop talking.

d) **HOLD EVEN**—Don't push or argue. Just restate your position.

e) **POSTPONE**—"Let's discuss that later." Rather than avoiding the issue, you put it off until later (and maybe set a date and time).

f) **DIALOGUE**—Exchange information with the other person or group; understand what led to each other's views; communicate; look for common ground.

As a commissioner, you want to resolve the issue while demonstrating good community values such as openness, trust, empathy and teamwork. *(See also Conflict, Page 14.)*

WHAT TO DO IF YOU ARE ATTACKED

Recognize the attacker's feelings but don't escalate the fight. Ideally you'll stay in your commissioner role and keep communications open. Try these *(See also pages 77 and 47)*:

- Look at him or her and gently say, "Say some more."

- Say, "Thank you, that's an interesting point. Does anyone else have something to add?" Pick up your water, take a sip and look around the room at others (inviting others' reactions with your eyes).

- Write what they say on the overhead screen, whiteboard or easel, then look around the room and say, "Anything else?"

- "Do you have any thoughts on what to do?"

- "Is there something you would like me/us to do?"

- If the complaint is about some other group's actions, you might say, "I'd like you to get together with them and talk this over. If we can help that happen for you, let us know. If you try and you still seem to disagree, please let us know. Please let us know what you decide."

Try to avoid responses such as: "There's nothing we can do about that here. Anything else?" *(Page 47.)* This is a use of power and authority to win, to close out communications. It does not demonstrate listening, understanding or receptiveness. By demonstrating rigidity and defensiveness, that approach builds citizen frustration and resentment.

MANAGING DIFFICULT CHARACTERS IN MEETINGS

People in most groups can be classified as:
10% difficult characters.
70% unable to cope with difficult characters.
20% not bothered by difficult characters

The best way to cope with most difficult characters is to steer clear of them. But if you can't, try the following:

DIFFICULT CHARACTER BEHAVIOR	YOUR BEST ACTION
1. Hostile Aggressive.	Stand up to him/her but don't fight. Smoke him out; ask for an explanation; e.g., "What do you mean?"
Sniper, Exploder.	Let him run his course. Hostile people escalate battles so don't push (he will just push back).
2. Complainer and Whiner.	Don't agree or disagree. Paraphrase their complaint back to them so they hear it.
3. Indecisive: Analyst; afraid to make a mistake.	Give him or her data and a deadline.
Be-nicer; afraid of making enemies.	Point out what is good for the group. Don't push or show attention.
4. Unresponsive: Frightened or Confused.	Outwait them. Don't talk, but look expectantly at them.
Silent, Passive-aggressive.	Involve them by directly asking them what they think about the subject.

5. Know-It-All, Real Expert and Phony Expert.	Don't argue. Do your homework. Ask extensional questions. "Why?" "Is there a study?"
6. Irrational (or drunk?) Emotionally involved.	Set time limit. Don't argue. Let them run out of steam. Adjourn meeting. Invite them out to the hall (or to your office) for a private discussion
7. Asking inappropriate questions.	Paraphrase what he or she says.
Changing the subject.	Cut in and restate the subject.
8. Repeater.	Recognize them by writing down what they say on the laptop/TV, overhead, easel pad, or whiteboard. If they keep talking, just point to the written statement. Remind them that it is already noted. Ask, "Is there anything I should add?"

CONFLICT—MAXIMS

For the Commission

1. Catch the conflict early before positions harden.

2. Keep boundaries open. Keep information flowing. Silence or avoidance induces paranoia and escalates the struggle.

3. Involve related systems, people and groups. Open things up. Ask for help.

4. Try to change the context within which the conflict exists. Look at the assumed constraints; rethink the setting—both physical and procedural.

For Yourself

5. Don't stake out any ground (harden your position) that you aren't prepared to defend to the finish. This means you must be clear to yourself just what your bottom-line-walk-away-point really is.

6. See if there is another way to get what you want. There are usually many roads to Rome.

7. Ask yourself, "Do I really want this? Is it worth a fight?" Am I actually anti-big-government or is it just that I don't want them stopping me from fishing in my favorite pond? Is the issue really important to me, or is it the thrill of the chase and the fight and the win that I find exciting?

Notes:

_____

_____

_____

_____

Section 5

APPENDIX

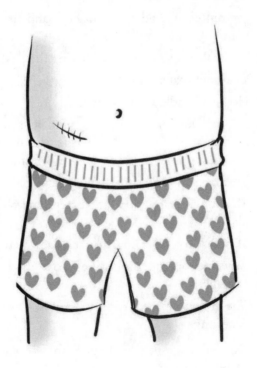

CHECKLIST FOR COMMISSION ORIENTATION MANUAL

Each commissioner should have a slim three-ring binder or website section with key information to quickly orient new members. The following have been suggested by commissioners. Check (✓) any that interest you: *(See also Page 54.)*

__ 1. Constitution and Bylaws—legal boundaries and limitations.

__ 2. Organization's purpose statement.

__ 3. Organization's goals and current plans.

__ 4. Budget and financial report, plus the Budget Process.

__ 5. Program descriptions/goals.

__ 6. Organization chart.

__ 7. Committees (standing or ad hoc) and their goals and plans.

__ 8. Any evaluations conducted during the past year.

__ 9. Personnel roster and Personnel policies.

__ 10. How to handle your expenses.

__ 11. All commissions or boards, with names and phone numbers. Also a list of key staff with names, responsibilities, phone numbers and organization chart.

__ 12. Meeting schedule and attendance policy.

__ 13. Meeting information: days, dates, length of meetings, place.

__ 14. Minutes from meetings for last fiscal year.

__ 15. Any appropriate procedures governing conduct of meetings.

__ 16. The follow-up reporting procedure on commission decisions.

__ 17. Outside resources including an annotated bibliography.

__ 18. The list of town council people, county board or other

group to whom the commission reports, or who rec-
ommends or appoints members of the commission.

___ 19. How to appoint/remove commissioners.

___ 20. Abbreviations and initials—the special language of the
Department.

___ 21. History of the commission—a brief narrative description.

___ 22. Thumbnail sketches of commission members.

___ 23. How to get things onto the Agenda.

___ 24. Upcoming key issues.

___ 25. Your legal counsel's interpretation of the Brown Act.

___ 26. Commission's major conflict areas or issues.

___ 27. Relevant town, county or state ordinances.

___ 28. List of commission's major accomplishments.

Others?

_____

_____

If your town does not have a Commissioner Handbook, be
cautious when suggesting or introducing the idea. Start with
just a few items. Others can be added later. The booklet
might begin with five to twenty pages and rarely exceed fifty
pages when complete.

It should be easily read and understood by new members—not overwhelm them. The commission should review
each page before it is added. Though written mostly by the
staff, it is the commission's booklet.

On the next page is the table of contents from one
town's commissioner manual or handbook. It is just an example. There is no one best way. The contents of your
town's Commissioner Handbook will reflect your town's
uniqueness.

COMMISSIONER HANDBOOK — XYZ TOWN

TABLE OF CONTENTS

Section 2, Commission Relationships

Relations with the Town Council

Relations with Staff

Relations with the Public

Section 3, Commission Effectiveness

Functions and Behaviors

Effective Conflict Management

Section 4, Individual Commissions

Planning Commission

Recreation and Parks Commission

Human Resources Commission

Personnel Commission

Transition/Waste Management Commission

County, Special Districts and Boards

ROBERT'S RULES OF ORDER

Robert's Rules of Order, first published in 1876 by U.S. Army Major (Colonel, then General in later editions) Henry Martyn Robert, were modeled after rules used in the United States House of Representatives. They are designed to control an adversarial or semi-adversarial process.

If you used Robert's Rules of Order with your spouse you'd be laughed out of the house. Similarly, you don't see them used in ordinary conversations, or by problem-solving teams in productive work situations. The motion-and-voting format hinders dialogue and openness, while setting a black-and-white stage that fosters contention.

Robert's Rules are commonly used in commission, board and council meetings. When used consciously they can foster openness and participation during the discussion phase; e.g., "I move we open the public-discussion phase and use the 4-Step Decision Process to understand the issues surrounding this application and to reach a consensus decision." "I second that!"

In the most difficult commission meetings, where opposing parties have fixed and rigid positions, are closed to dialogue and alternate views, and where a logical decision-making process such as the 4-Step Decision Process advocated here is not used, Robert's Rules can bring order and control. In these situations, however, the resolution of conflict is usually forced, so frustration and anger often remain.

Robert's Rules require first verbal, then written statements of what will be voted on, what the decision is and what will be done. This clarifies the outcome of a formal public meeting.

Look online to find many excellent summaries of Robert's Rules. Here is one at random: http://www.portlandoregon.gov/oni/article/22969

For a more informal, user-friendly alternative to Robert's Rules, try *Roberta's Rules of Order,* Alice Collier Cochran, Jossey-Bass, 2004.

Good luck!

THE BROWN ACT

"That which you do for me without me you do to me."
Jeffrey Brown (unrelated to Ralph M. Brown or California Governor Edmund G. Brown), TED talk

Government Code Section 54950-54963 states the requirements for a public meeting to implement the right of citizens to know what their public officials are doing. The Ralph M. Brown Act states the necessity for openness in public meetings:

"In enacting this chapter, the legislature finds and declares that the public commissions, boards and councils, and other public agencies in this state, exist to aid in the conduct of the people's business. It is the intent of the law that their actions be taken openly and that their deliberations be conducted openly."

"The people of this state do not yield their sovereignty to the agencies which serve them. The people, in delegating authority, do not give their public servants the right to decide what is good for the people to know, and what is not good for them to know. The people insist on remaining informed so that they may retain control over the instruments they have created." (Government Code, Title 5. Section 54950).

The provisions of the Brown Act are not intended to apply to less-than-quorum meetings of boards or commissions, nor to social gatherings where no action is taken or commitment made related to town affairs.

To function smoothly, commissions must develop good internal relationships, understanding, and trust. It is very difficult, if not impossible, to achieve this under the spotlight of formal public hearings. There is nothing wrong with meeting privately to discuss sensitive or organizational issues, though not the substance of pending items.

You may not agree with all of these commissioner suggestions.

1. **Download and read**: http://ag.ca.gov/publications/2003_Intro_BrownAct.pdf

2. **Adhere to the Brown Act**—Ask your town Attorney what it means in your town. If you don't like what she or he says, then check in neighboring towns for their Attorneys' interpretations. Announce at each public meeting how the Brown Act sets the stage for the meeting. Explain it as part of your formal decision procedure. This builds public trust and understanding. Announce in the local newspaper any large receptions where a majority of commissioners, board or council will attend.

3. **Hold Staff-Commission meetings** with less than a voting majority.

4. **Get together socially**—Don't discuss specifics; don't make decisions. Invite other commissioners, one at a time, to your home to chat. Get to know each other as people. Telephone other members.

5. **Call an Executive Session**—Use this for the topic you want to discuss (staff relations, what you expect from the Director, etc.). The public is excluded from executive sessions, and you can't discuss the substance of a pending issue. You may want to have counsel present.

6. **Hold a Work Session**—Use this to discuss issues or for an informational exchange, but do not make substantive decisions. These work sessions may involve staff, other commissions, elected officials, etc. These are commission planning meetings. They are publicly announced Work Sessions that deal with procedure only. Members of the public rarely show up at such irregular meetings, and usually leave from boredom if they do.

7. **Caucus before the public meeting** for ten to thirty minutes, to discuss how to handle an issue (not what commissioners think about it), or meet for dinner before the meeting. Some groups like to have their attorney present at such a dinner.

8. **Put over the public meeting** to a different but convenient other place, such as a restaurant or smaller meeting room.

REFERENCES

Robert's Rules of Order. You don't need all the arcane rules, just the general principles. The following link has more information than you'll normally need. http://www.portlandoregon.gov/oni/article/22969

The Brown Act. The State of California has a fifteen-page, very readable pamphlet for download. It's essential reading. http://ag.ca.gov/publications/2003_Intro_BrownAct.pdf

Looking for online resources? There are many. Here is an example for planning commissioners.

Planning Commissioners Handbook, Published by the Michigan Municipal League and specifically written for planning commissioners, this comprehensive and professional guide offers twenty-three pages of excellent practical advice for new and experienced commissioners. This free, online resource is highly recommended. https://www.mml.org/pdf/pcebook.pdf

The following three books are listed on Amazon. They cover more on the nuts and bolts of planning commission work.

The Job of the Planning Commissioner by Albert Solnit Paperback $31.95

Planning Commissioners Guide (The Citizens Planning) by C. Gregory Dale, et. al. (Planners Press 2013)

Planning Commissioners Guide: Processes for Reasoning Together by C. Gregory Dale, et. al. (Planners Press 1993)

4-STEP DECISION PROCESS— ALTERNATIVE LAYOUT

On the next page is a version of the 4-Step Decision Process that you can enlarge to tape on the wall, or to project overhead, for reference during your public meetings. Point to the current step so that everyone understands where the meeting is in the decision process.

For a downloadable PDF of this 4-Step Decision Process, send an email titled *"4stepfile"* to barry@ambiencepress.com.

4-Step Decision Process

1

Situation?
What is the
Issue or Problem?

2

Possibilities?
What are the
Alternatives?

3

Criteria?
How should
we choose?

4

Action?
What will
we do?

REVIEWS AND COMMENTS FOR THIS BOOK

BOOK REVIEW

Reproduced with permission: *APA California Northern News,* *November 2018*

Conflict, Meetings, and Difficult People: The Essential Guide for Members of California Public Boards, Town Councils, Commissions, Agency Staff, and Neighborhood Associations
Barry Phegan, PhD

Reviewed by Don Bradley, AICP, PhD

While titled "Conflict, Meetings, and Difficult People," here is a book that is equally useful to those who are honestly interested in hearing others' viewpoints in this complicated work of urban planning. The author has an architecture degree from the University of Sydney, Australia, a master of architecture and urban design from Washington University St. Louis, and a Ph. D. in city and regional planning from the University of California, Berkeley, where he also studied management. He has led many public meetings on difficult issues and during contentious times.

His short book (96 pages plus appendixes) is designed to help us work better with appointed commissioners, elected officials, agency planning staff, hired consultants, private sector business managers, organizations, and individual citizens.

It offers many tools to bring clear and concise communication to official meetings. Although California law states that interested parties are entitled to have their comments and ideas heard in the public forum, the law doesn't require that all stakeholders be treated fairly and respectfully. While "Conflict" suggests ways to address disruptive, rude, and difficult—or even threatening—attendees, it also provides pointers on running orderly and efficient—but participatory—meetings.

Many urban planners are members of the American Institute of Certified Planners (AICP) and are bound to its Code of Conduct. AICP members are tasked to be open-minded, honest, fair, cooperative, and reasonable. This book details how to include others in the effort to achieve AICP's lofty goals. Although this book is geared toward California—where the Brown Act regulates the ethical behavior of governmental officials—it might apply equally to other states. Dr. Phegan references (page 99) several documents written on the general subject of the planning commissioner's role. They include the Michigan Municipal League's "Planning Commissioners Handbook" (1997, 2006), "The Job of the Planning Commissioner," by Albert Solnit (1974, 1987), and the "Planning Commissioners Guide: Processes for Reasoning Together," by C. Gregory Dale (1993). While any of these may be helpful, they take quite different approaches from the book reviewed here.

Dr. Phegan reinforces that planning and implementing focused and orderly decision and meeting processes will achieve the best possible outcomes in public meetings. His 4-Step Decision Process *(Pages 46-47 and 100-101)* is a jewel. It will help us in our decision-making and advisory roles, where we often are expected to solve complex problems and controversial issues without the appearance of conflicts of interest or ideological bias. Our colleague Naphtali H. Knox, FAICP (editor of Northern News), tells me he effectively used this decision-making process in a number of general plans prepared by his northern California consulting firm.

The appendix covers Robert's Rules of Order *(Page 96)* and the Brown Act *(Page 97)*. "Conflict, Meetings, and Difficult People," goes far beyond these.

I recommend this book for anyone who wants to improve meetings while eschewing and deflecting power plays.

Donald W. Bradley, Ph.D., has been an urban planner for more than 50 years. He is also a professor of psychology, a retired clinical psychologist, a retired U.S. Air Force Reserve officer, and chair of the City of San Carlos planning commission. Dr. Bradley has led Northern California APA's AICP Exam Prep course for 30 years. He holds a Ph.D. in clinical psychology from Pacific Graduate School of Psychology (Palo Alto University), a Ph.D. in planning from the University of

Michigan, and an M.S. in city and regional planning from the University of Southern California.

Conflict, Meetings, and Difficult People: The Essential Guide for Members of California Public Boards, Town Councils, Commissions, Agency Staff, and Neighborhood Associations, Barry Phegan, PhD. Paperback: $18.95. ISBN: 978-1-7322483-0-4. 122 pages. For more information about this book, visit **www.ambiencepress.com**

BOOK COMMENTS

Kate Sears, Supervisor, District 3, Marin County, California

This is a good, practical guide for public officials at all levels, enriched by real insights into how to manage conflicts and effectively explore common ground.

I particularly appreciate the emphasis on building relationships, creating a more interactive decision making process, and minimizing misunderstanding by recognizing the different ways each of us see problems and makes decisions. A helpful guide for those new to public service, as well as experienced members of boards and commissions.

Bill Ahern, Executive Director, California State Public Utilities Commission

This guide is as useful to agency employees as it is to elected or appointed public officials.

About the Author—Barry Phegan

For thirty years Barry Phegan was managing partner of Meridian Group, a Berkeley, California consulting company specializing in company culture. His book *Developing Your Company Culture* is available through Amazon.

He taught various professional management-related classes throughout the University of California, University Extension. This guide grew from some of those classes.

In addition to his earlier career as an architect in Australia, Sweden and Canada, he worked in the USA as a planner, as a manager in local government, and as a member of a city planning commission. He led many public meetings during the contentious times of the civil rights era when violence and handguns made some meetings scary.

Barry Phegan has an architecture degree from the University of Sydney, Australia; a Master of Architecture and Urban Design from Washington University, St. Louis, Missouri; and a PhD in City and Regional Planning from the University of California, Berkeley, where he also studied management.

Barry Phegan lives in Marin County, California.
Please send your comments and suggestions to;
barry@ambiencepress.com